AAT

TECHNICIAN

CW00621194

COMBINED **COMPANION** Unit 10

Managing Systems
and People in
the Accounting
Environment

BPP

PROFESSIONAL EDUCATION

First edition April 2004

ISBN 0 7517 1775 4

British Library Cataloguing-in-Publication Data
A catalogue record for this book is available from the British Library

Published by

BPP Professional Education
Aldine House
Aldine Place
London W12 8AW

Printed in Great Britain by W M Print
45-47 Frederick Street
Walsall, West Midlands
WS2 9NE

We are grateful to the AAT for permission to reproduce their sample simulation. The answers have been prepared by BPP Professional Education.

CONTENTS

INTRODUCTION

This is the first edition of BPP's Combined Companion for AAT Technician Unit 10, Managing Systems and People in the Accounting Environment. It has been carefully designed to enable students to practise all aspects of the requirements of the Standards of Competence and performance criteria, and ultimately to produce a successful project.

The Course Companion chapters contain these key features

- clear, step by step explanation of the topic

- logical progression and linking from one chapter to the next

- numerous illustration and practical examples

- interactive activities within the text itself, with answers supplied

- a bank of questions of varying complexity again with answers supplied at the back of the book

- project notes, suggesting how to put techniques into practice in the context of your own project

The Revision Companion section contains

- graded activities corresponding to each chapter of the Course Companion, with answers

- the AAT's sample simulation for Unit 10, with suggested approach and answers prepared by BPP Professional Education.

The emphasis in all activities and questions is on practical application of the skills acquired.

UNIT 10 STANDARDS OF COMPETENCE

The structure of the Standards for Unit 10

The Unit commences with a statement of the knowledge and understanding which underpin competence in the Unit's elements.

The Unit of Competence is then divided into elements of competence describing activities which the individual should be able to perform.

Each element includes:

(a) A set of performance criteria. This defines what constitutes competent performance.

(b) A range statement. This defines the situations, contexts, methods etc in which competence should be displayed.

(c) Evidence requirements. These state that competence must be demonstrated consistently, over an appropriate time scale with evidence of performance being provided from the appropriate sources.

(d) Sources of evidence. In Unit 10, evidence requirements are closely linked to the assessment strategy. You are required to write a 4,000 word report based on an accounting system.

The elements of competence for Unit 10 *Managing Systems and People in an Accounting Environment* are set out below. Knowledge and understanding required for the unit as a whole are listed first, followed by the performance criteria and range statements for each element. Performance criteria are cross-referenced below to chapters in this Unit 10 *Managing Systems and People in an Accounting Environment* Combined Companion.

Unit 10 Managing Systems and People in the Accounting Environment

Unit Commentary

This unit is about your role as a manager in the accounting environment, whether you are a line manager or are managing a particular function or project.

The first element requires you to show that you co-ordinate work activities effectively within the accounting environment. This includes setting realistic objectives, targets and deadlines and managing people in such a way that these can be met. You also need to show that you prepare contingency plans to cover a variety of problems that can reduce the likelihood of meeting objectives, targets and deadlines.

The second element is about identifying weaknesses in an accounting system and making recommendations to rectify these. This involves identifying potential for misuse of a system, whether this is accidental (errors) or deliberate (fraud). You are also required to update the system, for example to comply with legislative requirements, and to check that the output is correct after the system has been updated.

Elements contained within this unit are:

Element 10.1   Manage people within the accounting environment

Element 10.2   Identify opportunities for improving the effectiveness of an accounting system

Knowledge and understanding

To perform this unit effectively you will need to know and understand:

The business environment   Chapter

1   The range of external regulations affecting accounting practice (Element 10.2)   1

2   Common types of fraud (Element 10.2)   7

3   The implications of fraud (Element 10.2)   7

Management Techniques

4   Methods for scheduling and planning work (Element 10.1)   2

5   Techniques for managing your own time effectively (Element 10.1)   2

6   Methods of measuring cost-effectiveness (Element 10.2)   6

7   Methods of detecting fraud within accounting systems (Element 10.2)   7

8   Techniques for influencing and negotiating with decision-makers and   3
     controllers of resources (Element 10.1)

Management Principles and Theory

9   Principles of supervision and delegation (Element 10.1)   3

10   Principles of fostering effective working relationships,   3
     building teams and motivating staff (Element 10.1)

The Organisation

11   How the accounting systems of an organisation are affected by its organisational   1,6
     structure, its Management Information Systems, its administrative systems and
     procedures and the nature of its business transactions(Elements 10.1 & 10.2)

12   The overview of the organisation's business and its critical external relationships   1,6
     (customers/clients, suppliers, etc.) (Elements 10.1 & 10.2)

13   The purpose, structure and organisation of the accounting function and its   1
     relationships with other functions within the organisation (Element 10.2)

14   Who controls the supply of resources (equipment, materials, information and   1
     people) within the organisation (Element 10.1)

Element 10.1 Co-ordinate work activities within the accounting environment

Performance criteria

In order to perform this element successfully you need to: **Chapter**

10.1.A	Plan work activities to make the optimum use of resources and to ensure that work is completed within agreed timescales	2
10.1.B	Review the competence of individuals undertakin5g work activities and arrange the necessary training	4
10.1.C	Prepare, in collaboration with 3management, contingency plans to meet possible emergencies	5
10.1.D	Communicate work methods and schedules to colleagues in ways that help them to understand what is expected of them	3
10.1.E	Monitor work activities sufficiently closely to ensure that quality standards are being met	3
10.1.F	Co-ordinate work activities effectively and in accordance with work plans and contingency plans	3 , 5
10.1.G	Encourage colleagues to report to you promptly any problems and queries that are beyond their authority or expertise to resolve, and resolve these where they are within your authority and expertise	Throughout
10.1.H	Refer problems and queries to the appropriate person where resolution is beyond your authority or expertise	Throughout

Range statement

Performance in this element relates to the following contexts:

Contingency plans allowing for:

- Fully functioning computer system not being available

- Staff absence

- Changes in work patterns and demands

Element 10.2 Identify opportunities for improving the effectiveness of an accounting system

Performance criteria

In order to perform this element successfully you need to: **Chapter**

10.2.A	Identify weaknesses and potential for improvements to the accounting system and consider their impact on the operation of the organisation	6
10.2.B	Identify potential areas of fraud arising from control avoidance within the accounting system and grade the risk	7
10.2.C	Review methods of operating regularly in respect of their cost – effectiveness, reliability and speed	6
10.2.D	Make recommendations to the appropriate person in a clear, easily understood format	8
10.2.E	Ensure recommendations are supported by a clear rationale8 which includes an explanation of any assumption made	8
10.2.F	Update the system in accordance with changes that affect the way the system should operate and check that your update is producing the required results	6

Range statement

Performance in this element relates to the following contexts:

Weaknesses:

- Potential for errors
- Exposure to possible fraud

Accounting system:

- Manual
- Computerised

Recommendations:

- Oral
- Written

Changes affecting systems:

- External regulations
- Organisational policies and procedures

ASSESSMENT STRATEGY

This unit is assessed by means of a project plus assessor questioning and employer testimony.

The project takes the form of a report to management that analyses the management accounting system and the skills of the people working within it. It should identify how both might be enhanced to improve their effectiveness. In producing this report students will need to prove competence in the co-ordination of work activities and the identification and trading of fraud in that system. Students may be able to identify weaknesses and make recommendations for improvement. All changes made must be monitored and reviewed for their effectiveness.

The total length of the project (excluding appendices) should not exceed 4,000 words. An appropriate manager should attest to the originality, authenticity and quality of the project report. The project should be based on an actual management accounting style, or part-system, within the student's workplace in the present or recent past. For students not in relevant employment, an unpaid placement such as a voluntary organisation or charity, club or society or a college department may be suitable. Alternatively (if no work placement is available/the student is not in employment) an AAT simulation in the form of a case study should be used as the basis of the project.

The Approved Assessment Centre's role

The AAC should undertake the following steps:

- make an initial assessment of the project idea

- use one-to-one sessions to advise and support the student

- encourage workplace mentors to participate (testimony etc)

- ensure the project is the student's original work

- use formative assessments and action plans to guide the student

- undertake summative assessment against performance criteria, range statements and knowledge and understanding

- sign off each performance criterion

- conduct a final assessment interview with documented questioning

The student's role

The student should ensure that the project's format is such that it:

- covers all performance criteria, range statements and knowledge and understanding
- covers the objectives set out in the Terms of Reference of the project
- is well laid out, easy to read and includes an executive summary
- uses report form style with appropriate language
- shows clear progression from one idea to the next
- cross-refers the main text to any appendices
- uses diagrams and flow charts appropriately
- starts each section on a fresh page

Note

The simulation will place students in a simulated work place role play situation, where they will be given a range of tasks to undertake. The simulation will aim to cover as many of the Performance Criteria and as much of the Underpinning Knowledge and Understanding as is considered to be feasible for the scenario.

Where all of the listed Performance Criteria and underpinning Knowledge and Understanding have **not** been addressed sufficiently by the simulation, documented assessor questioning **must** be employed to address any gaps.

All Performance Criteria and Underpinning Knowledge and Understanding must be evidenced.

chapter 1:
ORGANISATIONAL STRUCTURE

chapter coverage 📖

Element 10.1 of Unit 10 is concerned with the management of people within the accounting environment. In this initial chapter we shall be considering the background to that working environment in terms of the nature of organisations, their structure, the external forces applying to organisations and how this has an effect on the organisation, structure and workings of the accounting function within the organisation.

Throughout this chapter and the remainder of this Course Companion you will find points highlighted as **Project Notes.** These are brief comments on how the ideas being considered in the chapter can be related to the project that you will be preparing for this Unit.

The topics that we shall cover are:

✍ organisations and objectives

✍ mission statements

✍ organisational structure

✍ management information systems

✍ external stakeholders

✍ external regulations

✍ the accounting system

✍ the accounting function

✍ relationship of the accounting function with other internal functions

✍ resources for the accounting function

Element 10.1

<u>knowledge and understanding – The business environment</u>

■ External regulations affecting accounting practices

<u>knowledge and understanding – The organisation</u>

■ The impact on an accounting system of organisational structure, Management Information Systems, administrative systems and procedures and the nature of its business transactions
■ The organisation's business and its relationship with external stakeholders
■ The purpose, structure and organisation of the accounting system and its interrelation with other internal functions
■ The control of resources by individuals within the organisation

ORGANISATIONS AND OBJECTIVES

In the context of Unit 10 the organisations that we are largely considering are those for which you work. These may be manufacturing companies, finance companies, retail companies, firms of accountants or many other types. However it is also possible that you are not currently in employment and therefore have no current hands on experience of management, in which case an unpaid voluntary placement with an organisation or charity such as a sports club, playgroup, PTA etc may also provide you with the necessary material for tackling Unit 10.

However in this Course Companion we will be concentrating on managerial life within a company and therefore will start with some overall considerations about companies and their structure and purpose.

Most organisations, corporate or not, will have a set of objectives or goals - a reason for their existence. In simple terms this objective may be to be profitable or to increase market share or to be environmentally friendly in all of its operations. However most companies tend to have a variety of overall objectives and goals. These are often brought together in the company's MISSION STATEMENT.

Mission statement

A mission statement is a company's overall objective or the aim of the business's life. It may be a simple, one sentence statement or a more complex and involved paragraph. For example Thornton's plc, the chocolate retailer, states its mission statement in its 2002 annual report as 'To be the UKs leading retailer and distributer of sweet special foods'.

A further example of a mission statement is that of British Telecom:

'To generate shareholder value by seizing opportunities in the communication market world-wide, building on our current business and focusing on high growth segments, while playing our part in the community and achieving the highest standards of integrity, customer satisfaction and employee motivation'.

Perhaps one of the most famous mission statements of all was that of the Starship Enterprise in Star Trek:

' Space, the Final Frontier .... These are the voyages of the Starship Enterprise. Its five year mission: To explore strange new worlds, to seek out new life and new civilisation, to boldly go where no man has gone before'.

Project note

Whatever the organisation, the mission statement is a starting point for the organisation's strategies and plans. The mission statement is at the top of the planning level but as a manager further down the organisation your plans will always be in line with the objectives of that mission statement. When writing your project it is always worth bearing in mind the overall mission statement of your organisation.

Activity 1

What is the mission statement of your organisation? You may be able to find this on the organisation's website or from the latest set of published financial statements.

Strategies, policies and detailed planning

Part of your role as a manager will be to carry out planning exercises for your area of responsibility within the organisation. Strategies, policies and budgets will stem from the mission statement, and will be the context within which your planning will take place. These areas will be considered in more detail in Chapter 2 of this book.

ORGANISATIONAL STRUCTURE

Organisations tend to be made up of a large number of people performing many varied tasks. In order for these people and these tasks to meet the organisation's objectives there must be some form of structure to the organisation.

An ORGANISATION STRUCTURE is the formal way in which the people within an organisation work together, for each other and as managers of others. It will indicate levels of authority and responsibility as well as lines of communication. The structure should make clear who performs which tasks, who they are doing those tasks for and the degree of their authority.

Organisation structures are often depicted in ORGANISATION CHARTS which are diagrams of how this formal structure within the organisation works.

Organisation structures and therefore their related organisation charts can take many different forms:

- vertical structure
- functional structure
- product based structure
- geographical structure
- market sector structure

Vertical structure

In a vertical structure the tasks of the organisation are grouped into types and each type of task is headed up by a senior manager or director. The organisation chart for a vertical structure might typically look like this:

As you can see with the example of the Human Resources area there will then be subsequent layers of management each responsible for one part of the area's tasks such as personnel matters and training matters.

Functional structure

In a functional organisation structure there is less emphasis on the personnel in the organisation and more on the actual work functions that are carried out by each area of the business. A typical functional structure in a manufacturing organisation might be as follows:

In turn the manufacturing function for example might then be split into its specialist areas:

student notes ✐

Product based structure

Many organisations produce a variety of different products which may be very diverse and in such organisations the structure is often based about those product groups. For example a diverse company which sells cars, distributes fuel and manufactures glass for windscreens might have its structure as follows

Geographical Structure

Some organisations may find that the most sensible structure is that based upon the geographical activities of the business. For example a wholesaler with operations in a number of parts of the country may have regional managers for each area who all report to the Managing Director at the Head Office:

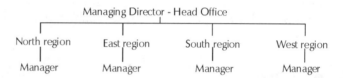

Market sector structure

In some organisations sales are made to very different sectors of the market, although the products may be similar. This will affect the way in which the organisation operates and the structure may reflect these market sectors. For example a car dealership may be structured like this to reflect the very different markets that are being catered for:

HOW IT WORKS

Angus Bell Ltd is a printing company. It is organised on a functional basis and its organisational structure is as follows:

Managing Director - Angus Bell

Printing	Sales	Purchasing	Finance	Marketing	Human Resources	Management Information
Printing manager	Sales director	Purchasing manager	Finance director	Marketing manager	Personnel director	IT manager
Neil Fraser	Susan Finch	David Keller	George Jepson	Katy Miller	Leila Franks	Kelvin Wells

Project note

When you are preparing your project it may be important for you to understand how the various areas of the business are separated and how they relate to each other. Therefore it will be important for you to understand how the organisation structure of the business works.

Activity 2

Can you either find, or alternatively draft, the organisation structure for the business in which you operate?

MANAGEMENT INFORMATION SYSTEMS

The reason for an organisation being structured the way that it is lies in the fact that the senior management wish to deal with the organisation in that way as it is logical to its operations. For example if the organisation has four separate regional sales units then it would be sensible for management to have information about the operation of each of those sales units. In contrast if a manufacturing company has one large factory but from this produces seven distinct products, information about each product is going to be the most important factor.

Management information requirements

The role of the managers in a business can be summarised into three distinct categories:

- planning
- decision making
- control

If managers are to carry out these roles then they must have the information that they require to do so. This is known as the MANAGEMENT INFORMATION SYSTEM.

Management information systems

The accounting function of an organisation will process, on a daily basis, a vast amount of information. Most of this will be required for the financial accounting records which eventually become, in summarised form, the financial statements for the accounting period. However the data input for financial accounting purposes, together with other data such as labour hours per period or idle time last week, can be combined and manipulated to produce information that is useful to the management of the organisation in their roles as planners, decision makers and controllers.

This provision of information for management in the format that is useful to them is known as the management information system. This will use both internal and external information to communicate to managers in an appropriate form the information that they require to carry out their functions as managers.

Project note

As a manager in practice, or in the role of a manager in your project, you will rely on the quality of the management information system to a large degree. This may be an element that you can focus upon in your project.

EXTERNAL INFLUENCES ON ORGANISATIONS

In the first few paragraphs of this chapter we have considered the internal aims and organisation of a business. However it must be recognised that a business does not operate in a vacuum and we must now consider external parties which influence the way in which the organisation operates. The two main external influences on an organisation will tend to be:

- external stakeholders
- external regulations

EXTERNAL STAKEHOLDERS

STAKEHOLDERS of an organisation are any parties that have a direct interest in the organisation, its business and the profits that it makes. There are of course obvious internal stakeholders who are the employees and management. However the EXTERNAL STAKEHOLDERS may not be so obvious. These will include:

- shareholders or investors
- providers of loan finance
- customers
- suppliers
- the government
- the community at large

We will consider each in turn.

Shareholders or investors

The shareholders of a company are the owners of the company and the people on behalf of whom the managers and directors run the company. In some small private companies the directors will also be the shareholders and therefore the direction which the company takes will be largely determined internally. However in larger public companies the shareholders may be institutional investors, venture capital firms or individual private investors.

In these cases the aims of the directors, in the form of the mission statement and strategies, may not always be the same as those of the main shareholders in the company. In some cases the direction of the company may be heavily influenced by the requirements of the main shareholders, particularly institutional investors and venture capitalists.

student notes

Providers of loan finance

Most companies will be financed not just by ordinary share capital but also by a variety of types of short or long term debt finance. The providers of such finance will have an interest in not only the profitability of the company but also in the security of the debt. The requirements of these stakeholders may therefore influence the manner in which the company operates.

The main types of loan finance and their implications for a company are as follows:

- long term bank lending - banks will be prepared to provide long term loan facilities to companies particularly in order to finance long term fixed assets. However as the bank will be concerned about the security of their investment there may well be stipulations in the loan agreement regarding the operations and financing of the business. The company will almost definitely have to provide regular financial statements and forecasts for the bank.

- bank overdraft finance - banks will often be prepared to grant short term overdraft facilities to companies particularly to cover short term working capital requirements. The overdraft is technically repayable on demand although in many cases will be a fairly permanent source of finance for a company. Again the bank, concerned for the security of the overdraft, will be particularly interested in cash flows and future prospects of the company and will require regular financial updates.

- debenture loans - many companies will issue debentures to investors which provide for a fixed rate of interest to be paid and the redemption of the debenture at some specified future date. Debenture holders can be institutions or private investors but in most cases the debenture deed will include a variety of stipulations such as how the company is financed in the future which will affect the operations and financing of the company.

- lease finance - rather than borrowing from a bank many companies choose to finance the purchase of long term fixed assets by leasing the assets from a lease company. Leasing companies have less direct influence on the operations of the company than banks or debenture holders but when a company takes out a lease it has a long term commitment to the lessee and the asset will normally be returned to the lessee at the end of the lease period.

Customers

If a company is to remain in business in the long term then it must satisfy its customers. This means that customers must be provided with the product or service they require, which they perceive to be of the right quality and sold to them at the right price. There is an increasing emphasis on the quality of goods and services provided to customers, with many companies moving towards Total Quality Management which has a significant effect on how the company is run and organised.

Suppliers

The suppliers of a business are important stakeholders of the business. As businesses move towards Total Quality Management and Just in Time purchasing their relationship with their suppliers and the quality of those supplies becomes ever more important.

Government

The actions of the Government affect the operations of businesses in many different ways from the requirement to abide by Health and Safety regulations, through dealing with employment law issues to payment of VAT and PAYE.

The community at large

In recent years there has been increasing pressure upon companies to act in the interests of the community and general environment as well as to make profits. This emphasis on social and environmental factors has forced changes in outlook in many businesses with mission statements reflecting not just the commercial aims of the organisation but also its social and environmental responsibilities. Just look back to the mission statement for British Telecom given earlier!

Activity 3

Give six examples of stakeholders in a company.

EXTERNAL REGULATIONS

The operations of a business, and particularly the accounting practices and function, are also significantly affected by a variety of external regulations.

The main regulations to be aware of for Unit 10 are:

- Company law regulations
- UK accounting regulations
- International accounting regulations
- Auditing regulations
- Stock exchange regulations
- Taxation regulations

Company law regulations

The UK Companies Act requires that all limited companies produce annual financial statements for their shareholders, in a certain timescale, in set formats and with detailed disclosure requirements. These regulations affect not only the nature of the accounting records that are kept but also the detailed timing of the production of the financial statements for the year.

UK accounting regulations

In the UK the standard setting process is headed by the Financial Reporting Council which guides and finances the setting of accounting standards. The accounting standards themselves, FINANCIAL REPORTING STANDARDS (FRSs), are set by the Accounting Standards Board. These FRSs and some older Statements of Standard Accounting Practice (SSAPs) set out the required accounting treatment for all areas of financial reporting and must be followed by limited companies. These accounting standards will therefore affect the type of accounting information that is recorded and the treatment of various items in the company's annual financial statements.

International acounting regulations

As well as UK accounting standards (FRSs and SSAPs) the International Accounting Standards Committee also produces INTERNATIONAL ACCOUNTING STANDARDS (IASs) and INTERNATIONAL FINANCIAL REPORTING STANDARDS (IFRSs). The importance of these for UK companies is that there is a move towards international harmonisation of accounting standards and by 2005 many UK companies will be required to produce their annual financial statements in accordance with International Accounting Standards.

Auditing regulations

Company law in the UK requires that the annual financial statements for all companies must be audited. An AUDIT is an independent examination of the financial statements with the outcome of an expression of opinion on whether those statements present a 'true and fair view' and whether they comply with the Companies Act. In practice this means that an independent firm of auditors must be employed who will examine the financial statements and prepare a report to the shareholders of the company regarding whether the statements show a true and fair view.

Under company law the accounts department staff must provide the auditors with any information that they require in order to carry out the audit and produce the audit report.

Stock exchange regulations

Public limited companies whose shares are traded on the Stock Exchange must satisfy further requirements which will affect accounting procedures and practices. These regulations not only affect matters which must be disclosed in the financial statements but also factors such as the internal controls within the organisation which tend to directly affect the work of the accounting function.

Taxation regulations

As well as the annual payment of Corporation Tax the two main areas where accounting procedures will be affected by taxation regulations are for the PAYE system and VAT.

The payroll function will need to ensure that monthly payments are correctly made to the Inland Revenue for PAYE and National Insurance contributions as well as keeping statutory records such as P11s and submitting returns such as P11D and P35 etc.

If a company is registered for VAT then it will normally be required to make a quarterly return to Customs and Excise together with payment of the amount of VAT due for the period.

Both of these types of taxation payments and returns must be produced on time and therefore will not only affect the type of work in the accounting function but also the precise timing of that work.

Project note

When considering your project you should put some thought to how both external stakeholders and external regulations affect the operations, procedures and working practices within the accounting function of your organisation. A particular current development that you might wish to consider if the impact that the introduction of International Accounting Standards might have on your role and that of others in the accounting function

Activity 4

Why might International Accounting Standards be an important external influence for a UK company?

THE ACCOUNTING SYSTEM AND THE ACCOUNTING FUCTION

We will now turn to consideration of the accounting system of an organisation and relate that to the accounting function itself. You may well have worked within the accounting department of your organisation for some time but may not have stopped to think about its purpose, its structure and in particular the relations with other internal functions of the organisation.

The accounting system

The ACCOUNTING SYSTEM of an organisation is designed to ensure that all transactions are processed accurately, completely and securely and that they are used to provide accurate information for both financial accounting purposes and for management information purposes.

The actual design and complexity of an accounting system will be dependent upon the type of organisation. In a **small business** the accounting system may centre around an analysed cash book and lists of customers' invoices and suppliers' invoices. In a **larger organisation** there will be a much more complex accounting system which will be designed to provide more detailed information. In a **manufacturing business** not only must the accounting system be able to produce the information required for the financial accounts but it must also be able to provide detailed costing information regarding the costs of manufacturing individual products. In a **service business** the design of the accounting system will be focused towards the recording of employee hours for particular jobs or clients rather than costings of products.

The accounting function

The ACCOUNTING FUNCTION is the department or individuals who process the accounting information and work within the accounting system. The accounting function itself may be a centralised function with all accounts staff working within the same office environment or a decentralised function with perhaps a number of accounts staff in each geographical location each reporting to Head Office.

Purpose of the accounting function

The purpose of the accounting function is largely twofold:

- to process the transactions of the business and prepare financial accounts

- to provide information for management

The processing of transactions will be done on a daily basis and include sending invoices to customers, receiving invoices from suppliers, receiving money from customers, paying suppliers invoices and expenses, petty cash, payroll, ordering goods etc.

The provision of information for management can be in the form of regular reports such as weekly manufacturing cost analysis or monthly cash flow forecasts or can also be in the form of one off reports such as detailed costings for a new factory.

The important point about the provision of this information for management is that the success of the managers in carrying out their roles of planning, decision making and control will be largely dependent upon the accuracy and the timing of the information received from the accounting function.

Activity 5

Draft a mission statement for a centralised accounting function.

Structure of the accounting function

As we have already seen, the accounting function could be structured in a variety of different ways, depending upon the size of the business, the organisational structure of the business and the type of operations involved. However in a typical centralised accounting function it is likely that an organisation structure for the accounting function could be set up as follows:

Under each manager there may be a number of individuals who work either solely for that particular manager in that particular accounting function or work in a number of different functions.

HOW IT WORKS

Angus Bell Ltd is a printing company. It is organised on a functional basis and the accounting function is organised as follows:

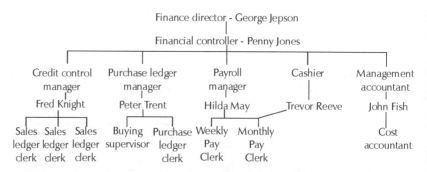

You will note from the organisational structure that the monthly pay clerk also reports to Trevor Reeve, the cashier, as her duties also include dealing with petty cash claims.

Project note

When dealing with your project you need to show evidence of planning and co-ordinating the work of those within the accounting function, so it is important that you fully understand the organisation structure of the accounting function.

Job descriptions

As well as knowing the overall structure of the accounting function it will also be necessary to know who carries out which tasks within the department. The overall work of the accounting department will be split between the jobs of the individuals who work within the department. A JOB DESCRIPTION should show the tasks that each individual is to perform, the timing of such tasks and the reporting structure for the tasks.

Project note

When planning and co-ordinating the work of individuals within the accounting function it is important to know what is required of each individual in order to meet their job description. This will enable you to assess each individual's competence to carry out their tasks and to assess any training that may be required to ensure that they can carry out those tasks.

Relationship of the accounting function with other internal functions

When considering the role and structure of the accounting function it is important to realise that it does not operate in isolation. Instead the accounting function is one of many internal functions within an organisation and it has relationships with many of these other internal functions.

Purchasing - Many organisations will have a separate purchasing function. This department will send purchase orders to suppliers on the basis of requisitions from other functions such as the stores department. The purchase order will then be sent to the accounting function to be matched with the supplier's invoice when it arrives.

Stores - The stores department will not only often raise a purchase requisition for materials or goods required but will also fill out a Goods Received Note (GRN) to evidence the receipt of the goods. The GRN will also be sent to the accounting function to be matched with the purchase order and eventual receipt of the supplier's invoice.

Sales - In many organisations there will be a separate sales function which liaises with customers and takes customer orders. The sales invoice will then either be raised by the sales function or the details will be sent to the accounting function for them to raise the invoice. The accounting function will of course have to record the invoice in the sales ledger and general ledger and also monitor receipt of payment from the customer.

Sales from stores - In some organisations it may also be the case that the sales department contacts the stores function with details of customer orders. The stores function then despatches the goods and sends the despatch note to the accounting function in order for an invoice to be produced.

Production - In a manufacturing organisation it is likely that the production or manufacturing area of the organisation will need costing information. The production manager for instance is likely to be interested in regular, weekly or monthly, variance reports regarding materials and labour in particular.

Senior management - The senior management of the organisation will require both regular and one off reports from the accounting function in order to carry out their roles of planning, decision making and control.

Resources for the accounting function

In order for the accounting department to fully function it must have the resources necessary to do so. Such resources will consist of people, materials, equipment and information. Many of these resources may be controlled by parties in the organisation which are outside the accounting function itself.

People - In order for the accounting function to achieve its purposes it must be properly staffed with the required number of staff with the required skills and qualifications. As a manager, one of your roles will be to assess the competences of the employees and determine whether training for current employees or the addition of new employees is required. In most large organisations recruitment is controlled by the human resources department but as a manager in the accounting function you will need to consider the levels of work for your staff, the competences required and the timing of the work. If the staff available do not meet these requirements then consideration should be given to a request for either temporary staff or permanent recruits.

Materials - The main materials requirements for an accounting department will be adequate supplies of pre-printed stationery such as sales invoices and credit notes, and items such as paper clips, staples, calculators etc. These will often be the responsiblity of the accounts manager or possibly that of a separate purchasing department which supplies all functions of the business.

Equipment - The type of equipment required for the accounting function will largely be desks, chairs, filing cabinets, safes and computers. As these are fixed asset items then there will normally be a policy in place for the requisition and subsequent purchase of such items based upon senior management budgets.

Information - The accounting department, in order to fulfil its own functions, is likely to require information from a number of other sources within the organisation - sales details from the sales department, purchases details from the purchasing department, stock movement details from the stores department, production details from the factory etc.

CHAPTER OVERVIEW

- all organisations will have overall objectives and these are often brought together in the organisation's mission statement

- in order for the people within an organisation to achieve the organisation objectives there will normally be a formal organisational structure which will often be shown in an organisation chart

- the precise organisational structure will depend upon the type of business and the nature of the business transactions

- managers require information in order to plan, make decisions and control the business - the provision of this information is known as the management information system

- there are a variety of external stakeholders in a business that may have a degree of influence over how the business is run - these could include shareholders, loan providers, customers, suppliers, the government and the community

- the accounting practices of a business will be influenced by external regulations such as the Companies Act, UK and International accounting standards, audit requirements, Stock Exchange regulations and taxation requirements

- the accounting system provides for the processing of transactions accurately, completely and securely in order to provide accurate information for financial and management accounting purposes

- the purpose of the accounting function is to process the transactions of the business, prepare the financial statements and to provide information for management

- it is important for a manager in the accounting function to understand the structure of the accounts department and the job descriptions of those working within the accounting function

---

KEY WORDS

Mission statement A statement of an organisation's overall objectives

Organisation structure The formal way in which people within an organisation work together

Organisation chart A diagram of how the organisation structure works

Management information system The provision of information for management in a format which is useful to them

Stakeholders Parties, both internal and external, with a direct interest in an organisation

External stakeholders Parties with a direct interest in the business but do not play a direct part in day to day business life

Financial Reporting Standards UK accounting standards which should be complied with by UK companies in preparing their financial statements

International Accounting Standards Current International accounting statements that are in force

International Financial Reporting Standards New accounting standards being issued by the International Accounting Standards Committee

Audit An independent examination of the financial statements of a company with the outcome of an expression of opinion on whether the statements present a true and fair view

Accounting system The system set up which is designed to ensure that all transactions are processed accurately, completely and securely

Accounting function The department or individuals who process the accounting information

---

CHAPTER OVERVIEW cont.

- the accounting function will interact with a number of other functions within an organisation either requiring information from those other functions or providing information to them

- for the accounting function to operate successfully it must be fully resourced in terms of people, materials, equipment and information.

HOW MUCH HAVE YOU LEARNED?

1   What is a mission statement for a company and where will it normally be found?

2   Explain what is meant by each of the following different types of organisation chart:

   (i)   vertical structure

   (ii)   functional structure

   (iii)   product based structure

   (iv)   geographical structure

   (v)   market sector structure

3   What is a management information system?

4   Briefly describe **four** types of external stakeholder and the relationship they may have with a business.

5   Give examples of **four** external regulations which may affect the accounting practices of a business.

6   What are the main purposes of the accounting function?

7   Give examples of **three** other internal functions with which the accounting function may have a relationship.

chapter 2:
PLANNING AND CO-ORDINATING WORK

chapter coverage 📖

One of the key elements of a manager's role is to plan and schedule not only his own work but that of the people working with him. In this chapter we will consider some of the techniques and practical aspects of effective planning and coordination of the work of those who are working for you.

The topics that we shall cover are:

✍ objectives, strategies, plans and budgets

✍ routine and unexpected tasks

✍ urgent and important tasks

✍ deadlines and timescales

✍ departmental planning

✍ project planning

✍ scheduling activities

✍ time management

KNOWLEDGE AND UNDERSTANDING AND PERFORMANCE CRITERIA COVERAGE

knowledge and understanding – management techniques

- methods of work planning and scheduling
- personal time management techniques

Performance criteria - Element 10.1

A Plan work activities to make the optimum use of resources and ensure that work is completed within agreed timescales

F Coordinate work activities effectively and in accordance with work plans and contingencies plans

OBJECTIVES, STRATEGIES, PLANS AND BUDGETS

In the previous chapter we considered the fact that organisations will have an overall set of objectives which will often be in the form of the mission statement. In a company context these objectives are the highest level of management planning and will normally have been set by the Board of Directors. However these objectives must then be considered in order to determine the way in which the company can achieve them. Again this will normally be done at Board level and the outcome should be the strategy of the business.

Objectives and strategies

The OBJECTIVES of the business are the overall aims of the business. For example a business might have the objective of 'year on year growth in market share'. The senior management of the business must then consider how this objective can be achieved. For example an increase in market share could be achieved by lowering selling prices to undercut the price of competitors, increasing the public's perception of the quality of the product by extensive advertising or by purchasing other companies in this market sector.

The choice of method of achieving the stated objective will be determined by the highest levels of management and will become the STRATEGY of the company, the means of achieving the objective.

Strategies and plans

Once the strategy of the company has been determined the senior management will be involved in determining the plans to take that strategy forward. Therefore if the strategy of the company is to achieve an increase in market share by acquisition of other companies, the next stage in the planning process is to determine how such companies will be identified.

Budgets

The next stage in the planning process is for management at many levels to determine the detailed budgets that support the plans that in turn support the strategy and objectives.

BUDGETS are the detailed plans of a business which are largely set out in financial terms. Budgets are a formal statement of the expected results of the business. Budgets will be set for all levels of the business and are objectives for that area of the business. Budgets can also be viewed as the maximum amount an area of the business might spend but in essence the budget is a management tool by which the actual performance of each area of the business can be compared to the expected performance.

HOW IT WORKS

Angus Bell Ltd, the printing company, has a mission statement which includes the following objective:

'To increase overall profitability whilst maintaining the quality of product and service to existing customers and new customers'.

The strategy of the company to meet this objective is to increase overall profitability by maintaining, but not increasing, price levels and by reducing costs wherever possible whilst not affecting the quality of the products or service.

The plans to achieve this strategy are cost reduction exercises for all significant products and areas of the business. In particular stores department costs are being reduced by a just in time policy of purchasing from only six major suppliers, with quality assurances. Product costs are being reduced by carrying out reviews of non-value adding costs for each major product line.

Project note

When producing your report you must always consider it within the context of the overall objective of the business, the specific strategies of the business and the particular plans and budgets that are relevant to your section of the business.

Activity 1

Briefly explain the difference between an objective and a strategy.

MANAGEMENT PLANNING

In this section of chapter we will consider your planning skills as a manager in order to satisfy Performance Criteria 10.1 A 'Work activities are planned in order to optimise the use of resources and ensure the completion of work within agreed timescales'.

Project note

Not only will this planning be evidenced in the content of your report but the fact that you have planned your report and completed it on time will also provide further evidence of this Performance Criterion.

Organising the team

As a manager in charge of a team, whether this is your regular team that report to you or a special one off project team, it is important that you ensure that each member of the team is performing the correct tasks in the correct order. The allocation of tasks to each member of the team is vital to the performance of the team and therefore is an important element of the manager's job.

Routine tasks and unexpected tasks

The tasks that must be carried out by individuals and by the team in total will be both routine tasks and unexpected tasks. ROUTINE TASKS are those tasks that the employees carry out on a daily, weekly or monthly basis as part of their routine job. UNEXPECTED TASKS are other tasks that are required to be carried out but are not part of the daily/weekly/monthly routine.

Both routine tasks and unexpected tasks must be undertaken but the question is in which order.

Activity 2

Explain what is meant by a routine task and an unexpected task and give two examples of each

Urgent tasks and important tasks

Both routine tasks and unexpected tasks can be classified as URGENT TASKS or not so urgent tasks. An urgent task is one that needs to be done for a deadline in the very near future. This is often because someone else in the team or elsewhere in the organisation needs the results or outcome of this task in order to be able to carry out their job.

Other tasks might be classified as IMPORTANT TASKS. These are tasks that are an individual employee's responsibility to complete but they may not necessarily be urgent tasks.

Prioritising tasks

Even with routine tasks it will be necessary to determine in what order those tasks must be carried out but when unexpected tasks are introduced as well this becomes even more important. This process of determining the order in which tasks should be carried out is known as PRIORITISING. So how does a manager go about determining the order in which the tasks of the team should be carried out?

Clearly urgent tasks are more important than non-urgent tasks. Equally, important tasks need to take priority over unimportant tasks. Therefore the tasks that are to be carried out can be split into four categories in order of priority:

Urgent and important tasks

These are tasks that must be done in the very near future and which are important. For example if the sales ledger manager is to produce the monthly sales ledger control account reconciliation on Friday afternoon, the sales ledger clerk must ensure that the sales ledger accounts are up to date on Friday morning.

Urgent but not important tasks

These are tasks which if not done will not be a major problem but they are necessary and should be done in the near future. If there is no coffee in the kitchen then no one can drink any - to some people it would therefore be urgent that someone went to the local shop to buy some coffee, but within the context of a busy office this may not appear important although probably good for employee morale.

student notes 🖎

Not urgent but important tasks

These are tasks which are important and must be done but they do not necessarily have to be started immediately as there is a little time before they are due. For example if the purchase ledger clerk has been asked to produce a list of creditor ledger balances (a two hour task) by Thursday afternoon for the purchase ledger manager and it is now Tuesday morning, it can be put off until Thursday morning if necessary.

Not urgent and not important tasks

These are tasks that are not required to done for any particular timescale. They must be done at some point in time but they can be done at any time when perhaps the team or individual is less busy. For example routine tasks such as packing up out of date files to be stored in the archives.

Activity 3

Distinguish between urgent and important tasks and give two examples of each.

Allocating tasks

One of a manager's important jobs will be to allocate tasks to individuals within the work group. Much of this will be common sense and will be based upon the manager's knowledge of the individual employees' skills, knowledge and capabilities. There are some general points to bear in mind:

- any specialist tasks should be allocated to those with the relevant specialist skills

- if an individual is the only person in the group capable of a particular task they should be allocated this task rather than other tasks that others can carry out

- some individuals may not like particular tasks so where possible the manager should be sensitive to this

- certain jobs may be generally unpopular although necessary, such as routine filing, so ensure that these jobs are not always done by the same person

Activity 4

Briefly describe what factors should be taken into account when allocating tasks to members of your team.

Deadlines and timescales

When allocating tasks to those working for you, the manager must also be clear about the timescale for the job and any deadline there might be.

A DEADLINE is a set time when a task must be completed. It is important to realise that a deadline will be set for a reason. Some are obvious reasons. The sales director has a meeting with a large customer this afternoon and needs a printout of the sales to this customer for the last six months. Obviously he must have the figures before he goes into the meeting.

Other reasons for deadlines may not appear to be so obvious. The financial controller has asked for some figures for Wednesday. The reason she has asked for the figures on Wednesday is that she has to write a report based upon those figures for the production director which must be on his desk by Monday morning. The financial controller knows that it will take her at least two days to complete the report.

Setting deadlines

There are few things more annoying for an employee than working hard to meet a deadline that has been set and then discovering that this date for completion of the task was an arbitrary date and there was no particular reason for that deadline being set. Therefore in order to motivate your staff it is important that only real and realistic deadlines are set.

Missing deadlines

As deadlines are set for a reason, if an employee fails to complete the task by the deadline then this is going to have an effect on the person or department that has asked for the task to be completed. In the two examples above, if the deadline was missed the sales director would not have the information required for the meeting and the financial controller will in turn most likely miss her deadline of producing the report by Monday morning.

There will of course be occasions when it will become apparent that an employee is not going to meet a deadline. This could be for a number of reasons:

- other deadlines mean that his workload is too much to finish everything on time

- colleagues who are providing him with information have failed to meet their deadlines to the employee

- he has simply not worked hard enough.

Reporting problems in meeting deadlines

Whatever the reason for a situation where a deadline is likely to be missed it is important to encourage those working for you to report this immediately to you.

This is important for two main reasons:

- You, as manager, or another colleague may be expecting the work that is being produced and may find that if the deadline is missed then in turn another deadline will be missed which must be reported immediately

- As manager you may be able to ensure that factors are changed in order that the employee can in fact meet the deadline.

This second point is particularly important. Provided that the problems in meeting a deadline are reported to you early enough there are things that may be done to help:

- you may be able to put pressure on any other employees that are holding up completion of the task by not producing the information

- you may be able to lighten the workload of the employee in order to free up time to meet the deadline

- you may be able to provide additional resources, such as extra computer time or another colleague's time, in order for the task to be completed on time

Specific timescales

In some cases, timescales or deadlines will be set by external circumstances and as a manager you must be fully aware of these. Examples of such external timescales which might be relevant to you in an accounts department are:

- *the financial year end* - this will require a trial balance at the year end, a variety of reconciliations and eventually the financial statements

- *quarterly reporting for VAT* - each quarter the VAT return must be completed on time and returned, together with payment, to Customs and Excise

- *monthly Inland Revenue payments* - each month the amounts due to the Inland Revenue for PAYE and National Insurance must be paid

- *monthly operating cycles* - in many accounting departments the month end will see an increase in activity due to sending out of customer statements, preparation of bank reconciliations, reconciliation of suppliers' statements etc.

Project note

In planning the work of your team or department, and in the evidence that you show of this in your project, you must be fully aware of any external timescales or deadlines as well any deadlines that you set yourself.

Activity 5

Why is it important to meet deadlines?

DEPARMENTAL PLANNING AND PROJECT PLANNING

In some instances as a manager you will be planning and coordinating the everyday work which goes on in your department as the line manager. However in other cases you may have been put in charge of a particular project which requires planning and coordination of the team activities.

Departmental planning

If you are the manager of an accounts department or a section of the accounts department then much of the work that is carried out in your department will be routine tasks. There will be likely to be deadlines that must be met for these routine tasks, such as sending out the day's sales invoices by 4.00pm each day or payment of all relevant purchase invoices each Friday. As a manager you must ensure that these tasks are completed on time.

It is likely that there will be unexpected tasks that are required of your department and this is where you must allocate such tasks to the appropriate member of your team and ensure that the employee has the necessary resources to complete this unexpected task in the timescale required. This may involve transferring some of that employee's routine tasks to another member of the department or freeing up computer time in order for the task to be completed.

student notes✍

HOW IT WORKS

You are Fred Knight, the credit control manager for Angus Bell Ltd. You have three sales ledger clerks working for you, Jenny Pitcher, Kerry Miller and Ben Noble. Jenny's responsibilities are largely for the input of all invoice, credit note and receipt details into the sales ledger. Kerry is largely responsible for debt collection and credit control and Ben deals with matching of receipts to invoices and most customer queries. All three assistants have experience of all tasks within the credit control department but specialise in those noted above.

At the end of each month Jenny is particularly busy as she is required to produce the list of sales ledger balances in order for you to be able to prepare the monthly sales ledger reconciliation. Just before the end of February, Penny Jones, the financial controller has asked you to prepare an analysis of the sales patterns to 10 of the company's largest customers. The obvious person to perform this task, which will take about two days, is Jenny. This however will mean that she will not be able to continue with her routine data input tasks for these two days or to prepare the sales ledger balances that you require.

One way of dealing with this situation is to allow Jenny the time to prepare the analysis required for the financial controller, whilst Ben inputs the daily data for Jenny and Kerry prepares the list of sales ledger balances required for the sales ledger reconciliation.

Project planning

By its very nature, planning for a specific project will require more management time. Most of the tasks in a project will not be routine repetitive tasks but one-off tasks required to complete the project. There may be a number of team members working on this project and a number of tasks which must be completed and may need to be completed in a particular sequence.

Role of the project manager

As a project manager you will have a number of responsibilities:

Planning the project - you will need to be aware of the start and end time of the project, the tasks that must be completed for the project and the overall result of the project that is required.

Scheduling the work - once the tasks for the project are clear then the manager must schedule the work required to ensure that all tasks are completed on time in order to allow subsequent tasks to be carried out and the project to be completed on time (covered later in the chapter).

Allocating the work - the manager must ensure that each task within the project is allocated to the appropriate member of the team (this was covered earlier in this chapter).

Coordinate the project activities and resources - the manager must be able to ensure that all tasks are being completed in the correct timescale and that all resources required such as computer time are available as and when required.

Monitoring progress - the project manager will regularly monitor the progress of each team member and their allocated tasks often by daily or weekly project team meetings. Where any problems are encountered corrective action must be taken by the project manager.

student notes

HOW IT WORKS

You are John Fish, the management accountant of Angus Bell Ltd. The company has been offered a large regular printing contract from one of the big London auction houses. You have been asked to assemble a team to produce a report on the anticipated costs of this contract. Today's date is Monday 23 February 2004 and you must have completed the report by Monday 8 March. You anticipate that once you have the information in place from various members of the accounts department team the report itself should take you three days to produce, type and proof.

The members of the team are the buying supervisor, Henry Philips, the monthly payroll clerk Sharon Gilligan and the cost accountant Ned Feltz.

From the buying supervisor you need costing details of all of the materials required for this contract, including any discounts that can be arranged for bulk purchase of the special paper required. It is anticipated that this will take Henry 3 days to accumulate.

The contract will require the permanent addition of a number of new employees together with training costs for some current employees. Sharon Gilligan is to provide this information and this should take two days to prepare. However as this is the last week in the month Sharon is busy preparing the month end payroll which will take all of Monday, Tuesday, Wednesday and Thursday.

Finally Ned, the cost accountant must provide details of the additional overheads to be caused by this contract. This will include in particular any additional stock holding costs involved in the bulk purchase of the special paper for the contract. Therefore although the overhead information should only take Ned 2 days to produce he will not be able to start on this until Henry has produced the information required about the purchase of materials.

As the project manager how you must allocate the necessary tasks to the team members paying particular attention to the timing of those tasks.

By working backwards you must have all of the information required for the report by the morning of Wednesday 3 March at the latest.

Ned will take two days to produce the overhead information and therefore must start this by Monday 1 March at the latest. Therefore Henry, who is to provide the materials information which Ned needs, must start his work on Wednesday 25 February at the latest.

Sharon cannot start her project task until Friday 27 February due to her other commitments but this gives her three days to produce the information and this should only take two days to produce.

Therefore your plan for production of this report might be as follows:

Wednesday 25 February (latest)	Henry Philips to start preparation of material costs
Friday 27 February	Sharon Gilligan to start preparation of payroll and training costs
Monday 1 March (latest)	Ned Feltz to start preparation of overhead information
Wednesday 3 March	Fred Knight starts to prepare report

Activity 6

Briefly explain the main roles of a project manager

SCHEDULING ACTIVITIES

Many projects that a manager is in charge of, either within the general work of the accounting department or as a one-off project, will be complex and spread over a fairly long time scale. It is therefore of great importance that right from the start of the job or project the manager is confident that it can be completed within the required timescale and knows how this is to be achieved. This can be done by detailed scheduling of all of the activities involved in the job or project.

What is scheduling?

SCHEDULING involves a number of related activities:

- determining the start and completion time of the project
- determining the resources available (people/computer time etc)
- determining the order in which activities must take place
- determining realistic time scales for each activity

- allocating each activity to the appropriate person
- coordinating the work of each individual
- reviewing the schedule and dealing with unexpected events

Once the order of activities and the identity of who will carry out each activity has been determined the schedule will be produced. The actual schedule itself may take many different forms depending upon the nature and complexity of the process. This could range from a simple list of start and completion dates for each activity to a large wall planner showing each individual task over a period of time.

HOW IT WORKS

You are Penny Jones the financial controller for Angus Bell Ltd. The company has a financial year end of 30 September but produces half yearly financial statements to 31 March each year. Here is a reminder of all of the personnel in the accounts department:

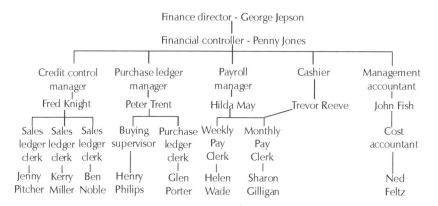

Trevor Reeve produces the initial trial balance for the half year financial statements and his timetable is to complete this by Friday 16 April. However before he can provide Penny Jones with the trial balance for her to produce the draft financial statements for the Finance director there are a number of other tasks that have to be performed.

Task	Time required	Employee responsibility
Preparation of summarised cash book for period to 31 March	2 days	Sharon Gilligan
Preparation of summarised petty cash book for period to 31 March	1 day	Sharon Gilligan
List of sales ledger balances at 31 March	1 day	Jenny Pitcher
List of purchase ledger balances at 31 March	1 day	Glen Porter
Sales ledger control account reconciliation	1 day	Fred Knight
Purchase ledger control account reconciliation	1 day	Peter Trent
Bank reconciliation	1 day	Trevor Reeve
Stock count	2 days	Ned Feltz
Accruals and prepayments calculations	2 days	Ned Feltz
Investigation of discrepancies discovered during sales ledger control account reconciliation	2 days	Jenny Pitcher
Investigation of discrepancies discovered during purchase ledger control account reconciliation	2 days	Glen Porter
Investigation of discrepancies discovered during bank reconciliation	1 day	Helen Wade

As well as producing the half yearly figures, each of the accounts assistants must also keep up to date with their other routine important tasks which will tend to take 3 days per week for each of them. Sharon Gilligan and Glen Porter will both be attending the college where they are studying for their AAT qualification on Wednesday 7 April for an assessment. Fred Knight is out of the office at a meeting all day on Tuesday 4 April.

The sales and purchase ledger reconciliations cannot be prepared with the lists of balances and the bank reconciliation cannot be prepared without the cash book summary.

Penny must now prepare a schedule to ensure that the initial trial balance is completed by 16 April. Due to normal month end procedures none of the accounts assistants will be able to start work on the half year figures until Monday 5 April.

Week commencing 5 April

	Mon	Tues	Wed	Thurs	Fri
Sharon Gilligan cash book summary	X				
Sharon Gilligan college			X		
Jenny Pitcher sales ledger balances	X				
Glen Porter purchase ledger balances	X				
Glen Porter college			X		
Fred Knight meeting		X			
Fred Knight sales ledger control account rec				X	
Peter Trent purchase ledger control account rec		X			
Ned Feltz stock count	X	X			

Week commencing 12 April

	Mon	Tues	Wed	Thurs	Fri
Sharon Gilligan cash book summary cont	X				
Sharon Gilligan petty cash summary		X			
Trevor Reeve bank reconciliation		X			
Ned Feltz accruals and prepayments	X	X			
Jenny Pitcher sales ledger discrepancies	X	X			
Glen Porter purchase ledger discrepancies	X	X			
Helen Wade bank reconciliation discrepancies				X	

Note: as Sharon Gilligan has to be at college on Wednesday 7 April and also has three days of other work to fit in then she will only be able to do one day of the cash book summary in the week commencing 5 April. The second day of this task must be at the start of the week commencing 12 April as the bank reconciliation cannot be produced by Trevor Reeve until the cash book summaries are ready.

TIME MANAGEMENT

A considerable amount of the time of managers is spent organising how the time of those that work for them is to be spent in the work environment. However it is also essential that managers, as individuals, make the best use of their own time. So in this final section of this chapter we shall be considering some of the principles of good time management and some practical tips on how to make the most of your time at work.

Principles of good time management

Set goals - break down your overall job into its specific tasks so that you know precisely what your work goals are

Make plans - make plans setting out in detail how you will achieve those goals - the tasks, timescales, deadlines, resources required etc

Make lists - at the start of each week and at the start of each day make lists of the precise tasks that need to be completed each day. Once a task is completed tick it off the list. If a task cannot be completed in a day add it to the list for the following day.

Set priorities - as we saw earlier in this chapter you will need to determine your priorities and which tasks are the ones that must be completed first.

Concentration - wherever possible try to complete a task once you have started it. There will be occasions where a task cannot be completed at that particular time and must be added to the next day's list but try to keep these to a minimum.

student notes✍

Urgency - it is always tempting to put off large, difficult or uninteresting tasks but make sure that you do them now and do not have to add them to tomorrow's list.

Practical tips for good time management

- be prepared to plan for the longer term

- in the shorter term produce a list of tasks for each day

- prioritise the list and tick off tasks as they are completed

- have allocated times for employees to see you rather than having an 'open door at all times' policy

- where necessary arrange regular meetings with employees where problems and issues can be aired, rather than seeing them on an ad hoc basis

- beware of the telephone - do not spend unnecessary amounts of time on telephone calls - be prepared to put the telephone onto divert if necessary

- Beware of e-mail - respond to any incoming e-mails that need your urgent attention but do not be tempted to reply to non-urgent or unimportant e-mails - be prepared to delete e-mails that do not require your attention

- as new tasks appear during the day allocate them to your priority list or delegate

- try to organise work in batches so that you are working as efficiently as possible

- ensure that you complete all tasks that you start wherever possible

Activity 7

Briefly explain the main principles of good time management.

CHAPTER OVERVIEW

- the Board of a company will set the overall objectives of the company and then will determine the strategies that the company will follow in order to meet those objectives

- once the strategies are set senior management will determine the plans required to follow through those strategies. These plans are normally expressed in financial terms in the form of budgets.

- it is important that a manager has planning skills in order to organise his department or team

- routine tasks are the general repetitive tasks that must be carried out but unexpected tasks may also be required of the team and must also be carried out

- in order to prioritise tasks it is useful to classify them as urgent or non-urgent and important or not so important

- tasks must be carried out in order to meet specific deadlines and also within other, often externally set, timescales

- deadlines should be met whenever possible but if it appears that a deadline cannot be met for some reason then the manager responsible for the task should be informed of this immediately

---

KEY WORDS

Objectives These are the overall aims of a business

Strategy The means by which a business will achieve its objectives

Budgets Detailed plans of the business set out in financial terms

Routine tasks Tasks that are carried out on a regular basis

Unexpected tasks Tasks other than routine tasks

Urgent tasks Tasks which must be completed for a deadline in the very near future

Important tasks Tasks which are not necessarily urgent but which need doing and are the responsibility of an individual

Prioritising Determining the order in which tasks should be carried out

Deadline A set time by which a task must be completed

Scheduling Determining the order in which tasks must be carried out, who by and when

---

- planning as a manager of a department or section of a department will largely involve ensuring that routine tasks are completed on time and fitting in unexpected tasks

- planning for a project manager however will tend to be more complex as there will be few routine tasks - the project manager must schedule and allocate the tasks, coordinate the project and monitor its progress

- scheduling activities entails determining the start and end of the project, the resources available, the order in which activities must take place, realistic timescales for the activities, allocating tasks to appropriate employees, coordinating the work of the team and reviewing the schedule for unexpected events

- a manager is responsible for organising the work of his team but must also be responsible for making the most of his own working hours - therefore a manager should have good time management skills and techniques.

HOW MUCH HAVE YOU LEARNED?

1   How do corporate objectives, strategies and budgets relate to each other?

2   If tasks are classified as urgent/non-urgent and important/not important how should these tasks be prioritised?

3   Give four examples of specific timescales that may affect the accounting practices of a business.

4   As a manager in the accounts department of a medium sized business you have been asked to be the project manager for a major report to the board of directors regarding the feasibility of opening a new factory in the Midlands. In general terms what would be your main responsibilities as the project manager?

5   As the accounts supervisor you are required to produce a schedule for the production of the year end draft accounts. What factors would you need to consider when setting this schedule?

6   What practical tips would you give to a new accounts supervisor regarding effective time management?

chapter 3:
MANAGING A TEAM

chapter coverage

In this chapter we will start to consider your role as a manager of people within the accounting environment. We will be considering your behaviour as a manager and methods of building, improving and encouraging your team of employees.

The topics that we shall cover are:

✍ the role of managers and supervisors

✍ leadership styles

✍ principles of supervision and delegation

✍ communication

✍ interpersonal skills

✍ team building

✍ staff motivation

KNOWLEDGE AND UNDERSTANDING AND PERFORMANCE CRITERIA COVERAGE

knowledge and understanding –Management principles and theory

- Principles of supervision and delegation
- Principles of creating effective inter-personal relationships, team building and staff motivation

Performance criteria - Element 10.1

D   Communicate work methods and schedules to colleagues in a way that helps them to understand what is expected of them

E   Monitor work activities sufficiently closely to ensure that quality standards are being met

G   Encourage colleagues to report to you promptly any problems and queries that are beyond their authority or expertise to resolve, and resolve these where they are within your authority and expertise

H   Refer problems and queries to the appropriate person where resolution is beyond your authority or expertise.

THE ROLE OF MANAGERS AND SUPERVISORS

Earlier in this Course Companion we noted that the main roles of managers within a business are threefold:

- planning

- decision making

- control

Within these three contexts we will now expand upon the role of managers and supervisors to consider in more detail what they actually do or what they should do.

Planning

Most of the planning aspects of management will take place at senior levels where objectives and strategies will be set. However more junior levels of management may be involved in the detailed setting of budgets for their department or section of a department.

As we saw in the previous chapter an important role of a line manager or a project manager is that of scheduling the work that is involved in meeting departmental objectives or completing a particular project.

Decision making

The line manager or project manager may have fairly limited decision making responsibilities but one important aspect of their role will be the allocation of the tasks involved in the work in hand to the appropriate personnel in the department or team (see Chapter 2). The manager must be able to give clear instructions regarding the tasks for each individual member of the team and must be able to coordinate the activities of each team member and deal with any clashes of priorities which may occur.

Control

Once the tasks of the department or team have been set the manager must constantly monitor progress to ensure that tasks are being completed and that standards of quality are being met. Any deviations from the plan must be identified and corrected.

Other elements of the manager's role

Apart from the three traditional elements of the manager's role considered above there are also other aspects that are viewed as part of the role of a manager:

- identifying problems in working practices
- developing systems for improvement of working practices
- innovation and creativity and communication of ideas
- support, counselling and advice for team members
- building team spirit

Departmental or section management

As a manager of a department or a section of a department the employees in that department will report to you as their single manager. All of these employees work in your department or section and you will be familiar with their capabilities and work practices.

Project management

If you are the manager of a project the team that is working for you may be made up of a number of specialists from different areas of the business. For example there may be a marketing assistant, a production supervisor and a designer as part of the team as well as members from the accounting function. The team members from the other internal functions of the business will continue to report on a general basis to their line managers in their departments but will also be reporting to you as project manager.

Matrix management

MATRIX MANAGEMENT is a system within an organisation where an individual reports to more than one manager on a permanent basis. For example in a geographical organisational structure the accounts supervisor may report not only to the regional area manager in which he is situated but also directly to the financial controller at head office.

Activity 1

What is the main difference between being a departmental manager and a project manager?

Supervisors

So far we have talked in general terms about managers. However at the lowest level of management there will generally be SUPERVISORS. The supervisors' role will tend to have the following elements:

- only a limited amount of their time is spent on management responsibilities

- most of a supervisor's time is spent doing his actual job

- the employees reporting to the supervisor will be non-managerial employees

- the supervisor will concentrate on day to day operations

- the supervisor will require detailed and frequent information in order to be able to plan and control the operations for which they are responsible.

Project note

Although your project is to be written from the perspective of a manager of a team, many of you will not in fact currently have management responsibilities. However throughout this chapter as we consider management techniques and styles you may be able to relate this to managers that you have worked for either currently or in the past.

The AAT Guidance Notes for Unit 10 make it clear that the project can be based upon either your own experience as a manager in an accounting environment or observing and analysing managers in action in an accounting environment or an AAT simulation in the form of case study.

LEADERSHIP

Whether you are a department, section or project manager or a supervisor you are a leader. This means that you have responsibility and authority for your team and most importantly the team members must recognise and respect that. Each individual manager or supervisor will have their own personality and their own way of doing things but it is interesting to consider some of the research that has been carried out into the different styles of leadership that individuals use.

Leadership styles

A number of years ago Ashridge Management College carried out research into different LEADERSHIP STYLES and identified four main different styles:

- tells
- sells
- consults
- joins

We will consider each in turn and you may recognise your own style!

Tells style

This style is also known as the autocratic style and is where the manager makes all of the decisions and then simply instructs the team who are expected to obey without question.

Sells style

This is known as the persuasive style and also involves the manager making all of the decisions. However this style of leadership is where the manager believes that the team members must be motivated to work properly and efficiently and therefore sells or justifies the decisions he is making to his team.

Consults style

This is a less autocratic style and is where the manager consults with team members but after taking their views into account finally takes the decisions himself.

Joins style

This is known as the democratic style and as the name suggests is where the manager and the team members make a decision on the basis of team consensus.

Implications of leadership style

The importance of this research lies not so much in the identification of the four styles of leadership but in the reaction of team members to each style. It was generally found that the 'consults' style was the most popular form from the perspective of employees although it was the 'tells' or 'sells' styles which were viewed as the most common methods of leadership.

However the most important finding was that for most employees the most important aspect was **consistency** of style as employees felt that providing they knew the manager's style then they knew where they stood as long as this behaviour was consistent. Having said this however it is entirely practical for a manager to have one normal style and revert to another style when the occasion demands. For example a manager may generally have a 'consults' style but in an emergency, for example an urgent deadline for an unexpected task, uses a 'tells' style.

Activity 2

A manager that you are working for on a particular project takes all decisions himself but ensures that everyone in the team understands why the decision has been taken. What type of management style, according to the Ashridge research, would this indicate?

Your own personal style

You may have recognised your own style of leadership from those detailed above, if you are a manager or supervisor, and obviously the style that you adopt will be that which suits your own personality. In practice however you will tend to find that your leadership style, as well as being governed by your own personality, may well also be influenced by the types of task involved, the managers that you report to yourself and the general culture of the organisation.

However it is important to remember that consistency of style would appear to be what employees want.

SUPERVISION AND DELEGATION

The knowledge and understanding for Unit 10 requires that you are aware of the 'principles of supervision and delegation'. This may sound quite straightforward but in practice many supervisors find both their role and the art of delegation very difficult.

Principles of supervision

Supervision is the act of ensuring that those employees for whom you are responsible are performing their work as required, to the best of their ability and within the standards and timescales specified by your organisation. In practice there are a number of principles that you should consider:

- **authority** - you can only supervise if you have the authority to do so - official authority comes from your position within the company ie accounts supervisor, but unofficially your authority comes from your leadership style and the way in which you conduct yourself. To be in authority over others means that you must have their respect. Authority gives you the right to instruct your team members to act as you wish.

- **responsibility** - with authority comes responsibility. This means that you are responsible for the actions of those whom you authorise to carry out tasks.

- **discipline** - as a supervisor not only must you ensure that those working for you behave within the standards required but also that you set an example of good behaviour and work practices.

- **merit** - individuals within the team must be praised or rewarded on the basis of their performance. Under-achievers should not be rewarded or praised, but possibly helped, whilst those achieving targets should be recognised.

Activity 3

What are the four main principles of successful supervision?

Delegation

DELEGATION is the act of authorising an assistant to carry out a task that a manager is responsible for. Although the assistant then becomes responsible for carrying out the task the manager remains accountable for the task being carried out correctly.

Delegation is an act that some individuals find easier than others to carry out but it is an important element of a manager's or supervisor's role. Delegation is important for the following reasons:

- it limits the work load of individual managers/supervisors

- it provides time for managers/supervisors to carry out their management roles, such as planning and monitoring results

- in some instances delegation is necessary as the task involved is a specialist task which can only be carried out by a specialist in that area.

Barriers to delegation

Many managers and supervisors find it difficult to delegate tasks to assistants. This can be for a number of reasons and again you might recognise some of these in yourself:

- lack of faith in the ability of assistants to carry out the task to the manager's standards

- concern about the effects of mistakes by assistants and the costs of putting those mistakes right

- a need to stay in touch with the workings of the team by carrying out tasks that could be delegated

Overcoming barriers to delegation

As we have seen delegation is an important management skill and therefore if individual managers or supervisors struggle with this aspect of their role then there are ways of overcoming this:

- ensure that team members are trained in such a way as to be able to carry out the tasks that are delegated to the correct quality standards

- ensure that there is full communication in both directions between the manager and the assistant as this will increase the confidence of the manager and the assistant alike

- ensure that the assistant is fully briefed as to the precise details of the task that is to be carried out.

Activity 4

Why might managers and supervisors find it difficult to delegate tasks?

Delegation in practice

The following procedures must take place if effective delegation is to happen:

- the task is formally assigned to the assistant and the assistant formally agrees to carry it out

- the manager ensures that the assistant has the proper resources to carry out the task efficiently

- the assistant is aware of the standard of performance that is expected in carrying out the task

- the manager monitors the progress and performance of the assistant and provides additional help or resources where necessary.

HOW IT WORKS

Peter Trent, the purchase ledger manager of Angus Bell Ltd, has been asked to prepare a report for the finance director, George Jepson, regarding the purchasing policy of the company and the number of suppliers that are currently being used. In order to prepare this report, Peter requires details of prices charged for six of the company's standard product purchases by each of the different suppliers used. Peter has decided to delegate this task to Henry Philips, the buying supervisor.

Peter and Henry have a meeting on Tuesday morning where Peter explains in full what information he requires. He explains to Henry that the information is required by Friday morning and that in order to free up Henry's time he will ask Glen Porter to carry out one of Henry's main duties which is the matching of purchase invoices to purchase orders and goods received notes. Peter has also agreed to meet with Henry on Wednesday afternoon in order to assess how Henry is progressing and whether any additional help is required.

COMMUNICATION

If a manager is managing a team or delegating tasks to assistants, it is important that the manager can communicate his views and requirements clearly. Therefore in this section of the chapter we shall consider communication within the workplace.

Written and oral communication

Communication within the workplace tends to take place in both written form and oral form. In either case it must be clear and fully understood by all employees.

The messages to be understood by those working for a manager range from the very general to the specific. In general terms all members of a team need to understand the role and objectives of the team and the systems and procedures that they must work within.

In terms of specific communication each individual assistant must fully understand the requirements, meaning and importance of any task which has been assigned to him or her.

Good communication

A manager therefore must ensure that he is capable of communicating the relevant information to all members of the team in an effective manner. This is not always as easy as it may seem and given below are some general points about effective communication in the workplace:

- whether communication is written or oral make sure that the right message gets across - this will often require some planning on the manager's behalf to ensure that he expresses himself fully and clearly - as a manager always ensure that you have the facts right

- ensure that the purpose of the communication is fully understood. Communication can only be effective if the communicator is fully aware of the reason why this communication is taking place - is it to develop plans? is it to monitor and control performance? is it to obtain information?

- the communication should be by an appropriate method and in an appropriate form. Should the communication be in writing or oral? If the communication is to be in writing is it most appropriate as a note or a more formal memo? If the communication is oral should this be face to face or over the telephone, in public or in private?

- if the communication is in writing ensure that it is pitched at the correct level for the person that is being written to - be aware of the knowledge and understanding of the person being written to and where necessary avoid jargon or overly technical terms

- if the communication is oral be aware of non-verbal signals that are part of the communication such as tone of voice, body language, facial expressions etc.

- be aware of the timing of the communication - if information has no immediate use or relevance then it will tend to be ignored or forgotten

- be prepared to listen to any feedback that is prompted by the communication - listening is an underrated skill but very important - listen attentively and actively - ensure that you hear what is being said to you and are not just concentrating on what you are going to say next

- ensure that the communication has been understood, that the message has got through and that action is being taken as a result.

Activity 5

You are the accounts supervisor and you have been assessing the performance of one of your assistants. You are not happy with their recent performance and feel that this should be communicated to the assistant. What would be the most appropriate method of communication and what factors would you consider before communicating with the assistant?

INTERPERSONAL SKILLS

INTERPERSONAL SKILLS are the ways in which individuals behave with other individuals. Delegating and communicating, as discussed earlier in the chapter, are examples of interpersonal skills or behaviour. Obviously in the workplace there is constant interaction between individuals and therefore the creation of effective interpersonal skills is very important. As a manager it is important that you can create effective interpersonal relationships and manage the interpersonal relationships within your team.

Effective interpersonal relationships

Effective interpersonal relationships are based upon not only an individual's behaviour towards another individual but also the way in which individuals are perceived in their role in the workplace. So interpersonal skills are not just about the way you behave towards others but also about how you perceive others and how they perceive you.

Why are interpersonal skills so necessary?

Interpersonal skills are necessary, particularly in a management or supervisory role, in order to achieve the following:

- understanding and managing the roles, relationships, perceptions and attitudes of members of your team

- communicating effectively with your team

- achieving the desired result from your management role

Ways of creating effective interpersonal relationships

There are many ways of creating effective interpersonal relationships and some of these have already been considered in the sections on delegating and communicating. However we will summarise the main issues again here:

- make a good first impression with your appearance, expression, manner, enthusiasm etc

- be aware of other peoples' perceptions of yourself

- try to perceive other people but beware of stereotyping

- be aware of body language - both the body language that you use and that which you perceive in others

- communicate clearly, accurately and with enthusiasm in whatever medium of communication you are using

- ensure wherever possible that you put others at ease with your manner and attitude

- listen attentively and actively to others and ensure that you understand what they are saying to you - this may be by the use of open questions which are questions which require an explanation as an answer rather than a 'yes' or 'no' answer

- try to recognise factors such as bias, ambiguity or distortion of any facts in any information that is being provided to you.

Interpersonal relationships within your team

As a manager, not only will you need to create effective interpersonal relationships with the members of your team but you will also need to be aware of the interpersonal skills of those team members and how this affects their work and their working relationships.

The interpersonal skills of individuals together with their individual personalities mean that there may be times when there are problems within the team due to incompatibilities which as a manager you will have to deal with. There may be compatibility problems in three main areas:

- with certain tasks
- with the management style
- with other team members

Problems with tasks

Certain personality types are more suited to certain types of tasks than others. Those with an outgoing personality and plenty to say for themselves might be good at working on the sales side with direct contact with customers, whereas a more reserved individual would find such a role difficult and stressful.

As the manager of the team you should be aware of the personalities and interpersonal skills of the members of your team and attempt to match the tasks allocated to individuals not only to their skills but also to their personality. However in some cases this will not be possible and the team member may simply have to attempt to change their behaviour or suffer the job in silence.

Problems with management style

We considered earlier in this chapter the fact that different individual managers would tend to have different leadership or management styles. Some team members may find a controlling attitude from their manager difficult to deal with, whereas others prefer to be told what to do rather than being consulted. In extreme cases a manager may need to consider changing or modifying his management style in order to accommodate the team working for him.

Problems with other team members

You will all have come across clashes of personality and this can be one of the main causes of conflict in the workplace between team members. As a manager you will need to try to sort out such conflicts and to encourage team members to understand the nature of their differences and to accommodate different personality types. It may be necessary for one or more of the team to actually change their behaviour at work in order to benefit the team as a whole. However as a last resort it may be necessary to remove a persistently difficult or obstructive member from the team.

Project note

In your project you may well be able to identify situations where there has been incompatability in any of the forms mentioned above and explain how you dealt with it.

TEAM BUILDING

A TEAM in the workplace is a formal group used for particular objectives. It will be made up of a small number of people who are committed to a common purpose and goals. These people may have different but complementary skills but basically hold themselves accountable for the achievement of their goals.

A team should be more than just a group of people. It is a group which has a specific purpose, a task to perform and a sense of identity. The use of teams is popular in the workplace due to their effectiveness in fulfilling the objectives and work of the organisation.

Types of teams

Teams can be formed for a specific, one-off purpose and this would be known as a PROJECT TEAM. In other circumstances a team might be a permanent working fixture with responsibility for a particular product or process and such a team will generally be known as a PRODUCT OR PROCESS TEAM.

Teams may also be either multi disciplinary or multi skilled. A MULTI DISCIPLINARY TEAM is a team whereby the members have different specialisms such as marketing and design as well as accounting. In such a team the skills, knowledge and experience of the team members are all exchanged.

A MULTI SKILLED TEAM is a team where each individual has a number of skills and can each perform any of the tasks that the team has to perform.

Accounts department and types of team

In some accounts departments, particularly in large organisations, the team will be a multi disciplinary team in the sense that individuals within the accounts department have their own specialisations such as sales ledger, cashier, payroll etc.

However in smaller organisations the accounts department will often be a multi skilled team as each individual within the department is capable of all aspects such as sales ledger, purchase ledger, petty cash etc. This is frequently a type of team that is to be encouraged, particularly by job sharing or job rotation (covered later), in order to be able to deal with situations such as illness and holidays.

Advantages of team working

There are a number of perceived advantages of employees working as a team. These include:

- combination of a number of different skills
- sharing of work load amongst a number of workers
- motivating factor due to fear of letting down other team members
- generation of ideas

Activity 6

What factors distinguish a team from any other group of employees?

Team members

A team will be made up of a number of individuals with differing characteristics, working practices, personalities and interpersonal skills. Research has been done in this area to determine the most effective character mix for a team and Belbin came up with eight roles which should be represented in a typical team.

Team member	Role
Co-ordinator	Effectively runs the team and provides overall coordination
Shaper	A motivator and one who spurs others in the team into action
Plant	Source of ideas and creativity
Monitor-evaluator	The analyst of the team who will analyse the ideas and spot the flaws
Resource-investigator	The social element of the team who can find new contacts and responds to a challenge
Implementer	The organisational force behind the team concentrating on planning and scheduling
Team worker	The diplomat of the team concerned with the maintenance of the team morale
Finisher	The one who has attention for detail and ensures that the team meets its deadlines

Building a team

Teams do not create themselves and there can frequently be a considerable period of team building and development until a fully functioning team is created. Tuckman has identified four stages in the development of an effective team:

Forming stage   This is the initial stage where all individuals are getting to know each other, the team objectives are being formed and the various personalities are starting to interact

Storming stage   In this stage the objectives are clarified and this may lead to setting of realistic targets and a degree of trust or might equally see a period of conflict within the team as relationships settle down

Norming stage   At this point the team will be settling down. There will be agreements regarding scheduling of tasks, quality standards and procedures for working.

Performing stage   This is the period where the team gets on with its work. Scheduling of tasks will have been agreed and the team project should progress.

Factors leading to a successful team

Some teams will be more successful and effective than others and we can now consider some of the factors within a team which will make that team likely to be more successful than others in its work:

- high level of commitment to team targets and organisational objectives

- effective communication between team members

- good understanding of individuals' roles within the team

- team members taking an active interest in team decisions

- general consensus within the team about decisions

- high levels of job satisfaction amongst team members

- high quality output achieved

- low levels of labour turnover

- low levels of absenteeism.

STAFF MOTIVATION

The achievement of organisational and team goals will be made all the easier if the members of a team are motivated to perform their individual tasks and progress the team towards its objective. However motivation of staff is an area which is fraught with difficulties and about which there are many theories.

MOTIVATION can be said to be the state of mind where the staff member is keen to achieve the goals of the team or the organisation as a whole. Individuals however will have many personal goals and the question to be asked is how is an individual motivated to work hard and effectively towards the organisation's and team's goals?

We will start this section by looking at some of the theories regarding staff motivation and then consider some practical aspects of motivation that you may be able to build into your project.

Maslow's hierarchy of needs

One theorist, Maslow, argues that individuals have a number of basic needs. These start from basic physiological needs such as food and shelter and then progress upwards through a hierarchy as follows:

Maslow's theory is that individuals will be motivated by each of these needs from the bottom of the hierarchy to the top. Once a need has been fully satisfied however it is no longer a motivating factor. So now we will consider what each need in the hierarchy represents:

Physiological needs - These are the basic factors of food and shelter

Safety needs   - Once the need for food and shelter is satisfied individuals then move on to require security, freedom from threats and a feeling of general order

Love/social needs   - After the basic safety needs have been met then individuals will be looking for relationships and affection and within a work and social context a feeling of belonging

Esteem needs   - These higher level needs are perhaps most relevant to the work environment and relate to recognition, respect and status

Self-actualisation   - Finally once all other needs have been satisfied the motivating factor for individuals will be fulfilment of their own personal potential.

Herzberg's hygiene and motivator factors

A further popular theory regarding motivation is from Herzberg. He recognised that there were two types of factors which affected motivation in the workplace.

HYGIENE FACTORS are effectively the conditions of work such as pay, working conditions, job security, company policy, administration, quality of supervision etc. Such factors will tend not to actually motivate employees but if they are poor or inadequate then they can cause dissatisfaction and be demotivating factors.

MOTIVATOR FACTORS are factors which affect personal growth and which do in fact create job satisfaction and motivate individuals to perform more effectively. Motivator factors include responsibility, challenges, achievement, status, promotion, recognition and personal growth in the job.

The conclusion to be drawn from this is that as a manager you should concentrate on improving the motivator factors such as responsibility and challenge of jobs for your team particularly where you are likely to have little control over hygiene factors such as levels of pay or working conditions.

Activity 7

Give two examples of hygiene factors and two examples of motivator factors according to Herzberg.

Project note

In your project you may be able to highlight ways in which you, as a manager, have been able to improve the motivation of those working for you. So we will now consider some of the practical methods of improving staff motivation bearing in mind the theories considered in the previous paragraphs.

Setting targets

When allocating tasks to individual members of the team a manager will often build in targets or goals for performance. These might be quantity targets such as the number of sales invoices to be processed each hour, or quality targets such as the maximum number of errors allowable. Getting a target or goal right can be a powerful motivating factor just as getting it wrong can be demotivating.

Specific not general	Employees will normally respond better to specific targets such as 'answering the telephone within three rings' rather than the more general 'answering the telephone as quickly as you can'
High but attainable	It is generally believed that a difficult target is a greater source of motivation than an easily achievable target. However there is a fine line to be drawn here as a high target may stretch an employee to try harder but only if the employee believes that the target is attainable
Agreement of targets	Targets or goals will only tend to be motivational if the employee has agreed to the target. If the target has been set by a manager but not agreed with the employee then the goal may simply be ignored by the employee
Feedback	If specific, high, attainable and agreed targets are set for an employee's tasks then again they will still only serve to motivate the employee to meet the targets if he is kept informed on a regular basis as to whether or not he is meeting those targets

Monitoring of quality

As we have seen, targets or goals are not necessarily about the quantity of transactions or processes but can also be about quality. When setting targets for individuals for the tasks that they are allocated it is important that a manager makes the quality of the output that is expected quite clear, as well as the quantity and the timescale.

Types of reward

It makes sense that a major motivating factor for employees is the reward they receive from doing their job. There are two main types of reward. EXTRINSIC REWARDS are rewards that are external to the job itself such as pay, bonuses and working conditions. INTRINSIC REWARDS are those that arise from performing the job itself and job satisfaction. These intrinsic rewards might include meeting deadlines, meeting targets, goals or budgets, producing a good piece of work or meeting quality standards.

student notes✍

Project note

As a manager of a specific team extrinsic rewards such as pay and conditions will normally be outside the scope of your authority. Therefore in your project you should consider intrinsic rewards and remember the power of praise and gratitude. Recognition that a team member has performed a task well or a thank you for meeting a deadline can go a long way in improving or maintaining the motivation of team members.

Job enrichment and enlargement

One of the main ways in which employees can be demotivated at work is if they are bored or are not being challenged. JOB ENRICHMENT is a method of building greater challenge, breadth and responsibility into an individual's job. This can be done in a number of ways:

- allowing team members greater participation in decision making and planning

- allowing team members greater freedom in determining how their job should be done

- providing regular feedback on employee performance

Another method of making a team member's job more interesting and challenging is JOB ENLARGEMENT where the job is widened by increasing the number of operations that the team member is involved in.

Job rotation

In many teams there will be specific jobs that may tend to be generally performed by just one person. This means that this particular individual is constantly carrying out this task and it might also mean that there is no one else in the team capable of carrying out the task. The effect of this can be that the individual becomes easily bored with the job and also that there is no one to cover that job when the normal employee is off sick or on holiday.

These problems can often be resolved by JOB ROTATION whereby employees either move from one job to another within the team, say every six months or a year, or each member of the team, whilst concentrating on their own job, also spends some time learning about and performing other jobs within the team or department.

HOW IT WORKS

In the accounting function of Angus Bell Ltd Ben Noble, one of the sales ledger clerks, is responsible for preparing the aged debt reconciliation each month and for assessment of any bad or doubtful debts. In February Ben agreed with Penny Jones, the financial controller, that he will take three weeks of holiday at the end of May and early June in order to study for his AAT exams. This means that there will be nobody available to produce the month end aged debtor listing and bad debts listing.

Penny has discussed this with Fred Knight, the credit control manager, and it has been decided that Kerry Miller, another sales ledger assistant will produce the aged debtor listing and bad debt listing with Ben's help in March and April so that she will be able to do the task on her own whilst he is away at the end of May.

Project note

When writing your project consider ways in which it might be possible to increase the motivation of the members of your team. In an accounts department, in particular, aspects such as job enrichment and job rotation are not only good for the employees but may also be a help to the department as a whole when employees are off sick, on training courses or on holiday.

CHAPTER OVERVIEW

- traditionally managers have three main roles - planning, decision making and control - however managers can also be said to be responsible for identifying problems and solutions, innovation, support, counselling and building team spirit

- you may find yourself a manager of a department or section of a department, a project manager or in a matrix management system where employees report not only to you but to another line manager as well

- the Ashridge research identified four main types of leadership style - tells, sells, consults and joins - the important point for employees is that the manager's style is consistent

- the main principles of supervision are authority, responsibility, discipline and reward for merit

- delegation is the act of a manager authorising an assistant to carry out a task for which the manager is responsible - this is often an area that managers find difficult

- communication between managers and their team is a vital element of the relationship and all managers should ensure that they follow the general principles of good communication

- effective interpersonal skills allow a manager to understand and manage the team members, communicate effectively with the team and achieve their desired result

- a manager should be aware of the interpersonal relationships of those within their team and be aware of possible compatibility problems with certain tasks, the management style and other team members

KEY WORDS

Matrix management This is a system of reporting whereby one individual reports to two separate line managers

Leadership style The way in which a manager or supervisor takes decisions and deals with members of his team

Delegation The act of authorising an assistant to carry out a task for which a manager is responsible

Interpersonal skills The ways in which individuals behave with other individuals

Team A formal group of employees used for a particular objective and committed to a common purpose and goal

Project team A team set up for a specific one-off purpose

Product or process team A team which is a permanent fixture with responsibility for a particular product or process

Multi disciplinary team A team in which the members have different specialisms

Multi skilled team A team where each individual has a number of skills and can perform any of the tasks that the team has to perform

Motivation A state of mind where employees are keen to achieve the goals of the team or organisation as a whole

Hygiene factors Conditions of work which will tend to cause dissatisfaction if they are not satisfactory

Motivator factors Factors which affect personal growth and create job satisfaction

CHAPTER OVERVIEW cont.

- teams may be project teams or product or process teams and they may be multi disciplinary or multi skilled

- research by Belbin identified eight roles which should be represented in a typical, succesful team

- the area of staff motivation is full of theories such as Maslow's hierarchy of needs and Herzberg's hygiene and motivator factors

- there are also a number of practical methods of improving staff motivation such as the setting of challenging targets, reward systems, job enrichment and enlargement and job rotation.

KEY WORDS

Extrinsic rewards Rewards which are external to the job itself

Intrinsic rewards Rewards arising from performing the job itself

Job enrichment A method of building greater challenge, breadth and responsibility into an individual's job

Job enlargement A method of widening an individual's job by increasing the number of operations involved

Job rotation A system where employees perform different jobs within the team or department

---

HOW MUCH HAVE YOU LEARNED?

1   What is meant by matrix management?

2   Briefly explain the four different leadership styles identified by the Ashridge Management College.

3   Managers often find it difficult to delegate tasks. How can these barriers be overcome in practice?

4   List as many general principles of good communication as you can.

5   List as many ways of creating effective interpersonal relationships as you can.

6   What are the eight roles within a typical team identified by Belbin?

7   What are the four stages of team development identified by Tuckman?

8   List nine factors that should lead to a successful team.

9   Draw a diagram illustrating Maslow's hierarchy of needs.

10 What factors should you consider when setting targets or goals for members of your team?

11 Distinguish between extrinsic rewards and intrinsic rewards.

chapter 4:
COMPETENCE AND TRAINING

KNOWLEDGE AND UNDERSTANDING AND PERFORMANCE CRITERIA COVERAGE

Performance criteria – Element 10.1

B Review the competence of individuals undertaking work activities and arrange the necessary training

STAFF COMPETENCIES

Before we consider the detail of assessing STAFF COMPETENCIES and training requirements we shall start with a consideration of the nature of staff competencies.

Types of staff competencies

Individuals within the accounting environment will require a number of different types of competence in order to carry out their roles. These will include technical skills, professional knowledge, administrative skills, computer based skills and interpersonal skills.

Technical skills

TECHNICAL SKILLS are the techniques, processes and skills that are required for an assistant in an accounting environment to carry out their tasks and perform their role within the accounting function. These technical skills will include:

- carrying out control procedures such as matching of purchase orders to purchase invoices or checking petty cash claims to valid receipts

- writing up books of prime entry such as the cash book and petty cash book

- double entry bookkeeping

- entering transactions into the general ledger and the sales and purchases ledgers

- performing sales or purchase ledger reconciliations

- performing bank reconciliations

- preparing final accounts schedules such as accruals and prepayments and bad and doubtful debts

- preparation of payroll and wages and salaries information

- writing up the fixed asset register

- writing up cost ledger accounts

- preparing budgets

- preparing variance reports

Most of these technical skills will be learnt whilst actually working, by teaching by a fellow colleague or a supervisor or manager. However other skills such as budgeting skills may be dealt with on internal courses. Many of these technical skills will also be taught as part of any professional training course such as AAT courses.

Professional knowledge

In an earlier chapter we considered the external regulations that affect accounting practices. These include the Companies Act, Financial Reporting Standards (FRSs) and Statements of Standard Accounting Practice (SSAPs), International Accounting Standards, taxation regulations and Stock Exchange Regulations. These are all elements of the PROFESSIONAL KNOWLEDGE that an assistant in an accounting function may need to carry out their role effectively.

Many of these regulations are regularly updated, in particular accounting standards. Accounts personnel will need to keep abreast of changes in professional regulations, particularly changes in accounting standards and the possible introduction into their company's accounting procedures of compliance with International Accounting Standards from 2005.

Many companies will use internal training courses to update accounts personnel as necessary, although in other cases accounts assistants may need to stay informed by regular reading of the accountancy press.

Administrative skills

As well as being able to carry out technical accounting tasks such as reconciliations and variance calculations, accounts personnel may also be required to carry out a number of administrative tasks such as the following:

- completion of monthly PAYE/NIC forms
- completion of quarterly VAT return
- completion of weekly/monthly time sheets
- preparation of reports for varying levels of management

Such ADMINISTRATIVE SKILLS may again be taught 'on the job' but there may be internal courses or internal manuals for skills such as report writing.

Computer based skills

Most accounting functions will be computerised to some degree or another and therefore all accounts personnel will require at the very least basic COMPUTER BASED SKILLS such as word-processing and batch processing of documents. An accounts assistant's role will often include the ability to use a particular computer package which the firm uses, or specialist applications such as graphics packages or spreadsheets. Such techniques and skills may be taught as part of internal training, 'on the job' training or an external training course may be required.

student notes✍

Interpersonal skills

We considered INTERPERSONAL SKILLS in detail in the previous chapter. Many such skills cannot be taught in a formal manner but as a manager you must consider the extent to which those working for you possess such skills and ways of improving them where necessary.

Project note

As part of your project you should be aware of the skills that employees working for you possess and also try to consider whether there are other skills that you feel that they require in order to carry out their roles effectively.

STAFF APPRAISAL

Although, as a manager, you will have an opportunity to assess the various skills and competencies of those working for you whilst they are performing their various tasks, a more formal method of assessing the skills, competencies and training and development needs of employees is a staff APPRAISAL SCHEME.

An appraisal scheme is a formal system where the performance of an employee over the past period is considered and any deficiencies and possible improvements are identified. An appraisal scheme may involve a degree of form filling and will almost certainly involve a personal interview between the employee and either their line manager or personnel manager. An appraisal scheme allows managers not only to form an impression of an employee's performance from their work but to be able to consider their performance and competencies in more detail and to discuss this with the employee involved.

Objectives of an appraisal scheme

Specific appraisal schemes for different employers will take many different forms but most will have the same basic objectives. These objectives may include some or all of the following:

■ to review the performance of the employee and compare to standards of performance set by the organisation

■ to identify areas for improvement

■ to identify areas where training or development are required

■ to identify what the employee must do in future in order to play a part in the realisation of departmental or organisational goals

■ to set out to the employee the results and standards of performance expected in the next period

■ to assess the employee's level of remuneration

■ to identify candidates for promotion

■ gaining agreement of the employee to the assessment of their past performance and the aims of their future performance and training and development needs.

The appraisal process

There are a number of important stages in any appraisal scheme and the following are typical:

Criteria for assessment - Before the assessment of an employee's performance can take place standards of performance and competencies required for that employee in their role must be determined. This may be based upon the job description for the employee or a job analysis. Only when the standards have been set can the performance of the employee be compared to the standards or required competencies.

Appraisal report - The next stage is the preparation of the APPRAISAL REPORT which assesses the performance of the employee over the past period. In older style organisations this will tend to be produced by the employee's line manager however there is a growing tendency for the report to be prepared by the employees themselves or by both the employee and the line manager.

Appraisal interview - The APPRAISAL INTERVIEW is the forum for joint discussion of the appraisal report, agreement of areas for improvement, identification of training and development needs and agreement of future actions.

student notes🖎

Assessment review - In many systems the actual appraisal and subsequent managerial assessment will be reviewed by a more senior manager.

Preparation of action plan - Once the appraisal has been carried out and reviewed, an action plan will be drawn up for the employee which will include plans for future performance standards as well as plans to deal with any training and development needs that were identified in the appraisal review.

Follow up process - This is the very necessary process of monitoring the progress of the action plan and the implementation of any agreed actions by the employee or training agreed by the employer.

Activity 1

What are the main stages of a typical appraisal scheme?

Appraisal interview

As a manager you may be required to carry out an appraisal interview. Although this may be routine for you this will be extremely important to the employee as their future within the organisation may depend upon it. Therefore the importance of carrying out the interview well cannot be underestimated.

There are four main stages to the appraisal interview from the manager's perspective.

- preparation
- interview
- appraisal report
- follow up procedures

Preparation of appraisal interview

As a manager assessing the performance of an employee you must ensure that you are fully aware of the performance of the employee over the period being reviewed and that you are aware of any relevant facts. You should ensure that you discuss the employee with any other managers for whom he has worked and also review the employee's history. You should also look back to the previous appraisal and determine how well any action plan made at that time has been carried out.

When all of this background information has been gathered the appraisal report can be prepared if it is the organisation's policy for the manager to complete the report in advance of the interview.

Appraisal interview

During the interview itself the manager's technique is important. You must ensure that you discuss the issues raised in the appraisal report rather than argue about them, and listen to the employee's views. The employee should be encouraged to talk about any issues, to identify any problems and to suggest solutions.

Any plan of action that is determined must, most importantly, be agreed with the employee. At the end of the interview the employee's understanding of what has been agreed as the plan of action must be clarified with the employee.

Appraisal report

It was noted earlier that in many organisations the employee fills in an appraisal report before the appraisal interview. This is then discussed with the manager and after discussion and agreement the manager will fill out his own appraisal report at the end of the appraisal interview.

Follow up

It could be argued that the follow up procedures are the most important part of the appraisal process. In many cases the completed appraisal report will be reviewed by the appraising manager's immediate manager and any problems that have arisen will be solved and any action agreed upon authorised. It is then likely that the report will be forwarded to the personnel or human resources department or the training and development officer.

There are however further slightly longer term follow up procedures which will include:

- ensuring that the employee is fully aware of the results of the appraisal and the actions that are to follow

- ensuring that the actions agreed to are carried out on both the part of the employee and the employer

- monitoring the progress of the employee compared to the training, tasks or standards set at the appraisal

- providing help or encouragement for the employee to meet the targets set where necessary

PERSONAL STAFF DEVELOPMENT

PERSONAL DEVELOPMENT is a much wider issue than simply training. Personal development may incorporate training of various kinds but it is also about the formulation of personal and career goals, the widening of experiences and challenges and the identification and planning of future opportunities.

Personal development plans

In the current climate individual employees are encouraged to define their own PERSONAL DEVELOPMENT PLANS or objectives. This should be done within the context of the individual's career goals and within the context of the individual's own abilities. It is generally thought that personal development plans should be, what is known as, SMARTER:

S   Specific

M   Measurable

A   Agreed

R   Realistic

T   Time-bounded

E   Evaluated

R   Reviewed

We will now consider each of these elements in turn to help you to develop SMARTER personal development plans.

Specific

This is the key to the setting of development plans or objectives. 'I hope to be promoted soon' is far too vague - 'I hope to pass my first year AAT exams and be promoted to accounts assistant (senior)' is much better. Employees should try to be exact about what they hope to achieve and break it down into small, manageable steps.

Measurable

One of the factors involved in personal development is being able to review an employee's progress and determine how the employee is progressing towards his goals. One way of doing this is to be able to measure how the employee is moving towards his objectives. Did he pass the last set of exams that he sat? Did the employee successfully complete the computer course he was booked onto?

Agreed

Despite the fact that employees might be setting their own personal development plans in many cases the achievement of these plans will require the commitment of resources from the employer. This may be simply the loss of the employee's time while studying or going on a training course, but will also encompass the direct costs of development. Therefore it is important that, where necessary, any personal development plans are agreed with the appropriate person which will often be the employee's line manager or human resources manager.

Realistic

When setting personal development plans an employee must ensure that he is able to achieve these objectives within the various constraints under which he operates - time, resources, ability and current commitments. The plans must be realistic.

Time-bounded

This element is tied in with realism but it is essential when setting personal development plans to include a time scale in which the plans are to be achieved. 'To be promoted to accounts supervisor' is the start of an objective but is this within a two year time scale or a ten year time scale - 'to be promoted to accounts supervisor within two years' is a much better development objective.

Evaluated

This will be part of the process of agreeing a personal development plan with the appropriate manager. There will need to be an evaluation process as to whether the plan is worth pursuing given the time, cost and other resources that it will require. This will often take place as part of the appraisal process (see earlier in this chapter).

Reviewed

This is an important aspect of setting personal development objectives. When and how will the employee's progress towards meeting the objective be reviewed? This will normally take place at regular employee appraisal interviews.

Activity 2

What does SMARTER stand for in the context of setting personal development plans?

TRAINING

As we have already seen one aspect of staff personal development is TRAINING. Training is more specific than personal development and encompasses methods of teaching or coaching employees to have the various skills that are required for their current jobs and roles.

Identifying training needs

An individual employee's TRAINING NEEDS are the skills that the employee needs to do both his current job and to progress towards his personal development objectives. However these are skills which the employee does not yet possess. These training needs will largely be identified during the appraisal process but may also appear on an ad hoc basis during the course of day to day work.

For example if an employee is seconded to a particular project team to carry out tasks that are not normally part of his job then it may become clear to the manager of the project team that the employee needs additional skills for this project over and above those he already possesses.

HOW IT WORKS

Penny Jones, the financial controller for Angus Bell Ltd, has had two training issues brought to her attention.

Ned Feltz, the cost accountant, has been seconded to a project team which is being led by the production manager to consider the financial implications of opening a further printing factory. As part of this project team Ned is to draw up detailed cost budgets for the factory at various levels of operation. Although Ned has in the past prepared cost figures for budgeting for the management accountant John Fish he has no detailed knowledge of budgeting and has told the production manager this.

Peter Trent, the purchase ledger manager, has announced that he will be taking early retirement in three months time. Henry Phillips, the buying supervisor, is an extremely competent member of staff and would appear to be the obvious replacement for Peter.

Penny must now ensure that Ned receives the necessary training on the subject of preparing budgets in order to fulfill his role within the project team. She must also ensure that over the next three months Henry is trained to carrying out the tasks and responsibilities of Peter Trent so that he is in a position to take over his role in three months time.

Penny has also agreed with the finance director that Glen Porter, the purchase ledger clerk, should take over the buying supervisor role from Henry in three months time. Therefore he must be trained in the buying supervisor's role in this period.

Methods of training

There are a variety of methods of training and to be effective for an employee the training must be of the right kind for its purpose. The methods of training that we will consider are:

- induction training
- on the job training
- training courses
- computer based training
- mentoring

Induction training

INDUCTION TRAINING is the training that tends to be given to new employees when they first arrive in the organisation. On the first day there may be an initial period with the personnel or human resources manager and then the new employee will normally be introduced to their line manager or supervisor.

The induction training will then follow the following typical procedures:

- explanation of the hours of work, lunch breaks etc

- explanation of the requirements of the new employee's job and the goals of each task

- explanation of the aims and goals of the department as a whole

- introduction to fellow employees and particularly any supervisor to whom the employee will be reporting

- explanation of the overall structure of the department

- introduction to machinery that may be used as part of the job such as computer terminals, printers, photocopiers etc

- introduction to the health and safety policy of the organisation and explanation of who the health and safety officer is

student notes✍

- assessment of any detailed training that the employee will require in order to carry out his job - this may include on the job training, formal training courses or mentoring (see later in the chapter)

- organisation of training programme for new employee.

HOW IT WORKS

The accounts department of Angus Bell Ltd has recently recruited a new cost accountant as the pressure of work on Ned Feltz is too great and the job needs to be shared by another accounts assistant. The new cost accountant is called Liz Spence and this morning is her first day.

Liz is initially shown to Penny Jones' office and is then introduced to John Fish, the management accountant, who will carry out this induction process.

John explains the following matters to Liz:

- her working hours are 9.00am to 5.30 pm with one hour for lunch and a morning and afternoon coffee break of 15 minutes each. Lunch should be taken from 1.00pm to 2.00pm as Ned Feltz takes his from 12.00 to 1.00pm.

- the requirements of her job are to produce weekly production cost figures and to help in the preparation of monthly management accounts. Each week she will also have to prepare variance calculations for cost figures.

- her reporting structure is to report directly to John Fish who in turn reports to Penny Jones, the financial controller. The head of the department is George Jepson, the finance director.

- the health and safety officer is Julian Smith who is the personnel supervisor and can be contacted on extension 2204.

John then shows Liz where her desk and computer terminal are, where the printers are and where the fax machine is. He then takes her to the photocopier, which is state of the art, and explains how this works although advises her to get help from Ned or any of the other accounts assistants if she gets stuck.

John provides Liz with a copy of the health and safety procedures and asks her to take them away and read them and to sign them as evidence that she has read them.

Finally they discuss Liz's previous experience and skills. It would appear that Liz has no knowledge of the computer package that the accounting function uses and therefore John agrees to arrange an in-house training session on this within the next few days.

On the job training

ON THE JOB TRAINING is a method of teaching or showing an employee the skills and techniques that are required for him to carry out his tasks. This will normally take the form of the employee being shown or instructed in how to carry out a task and then allowing them to get on with it. It is important that the employee is not left totally alone and that there is support available if the employee gets stuck. It is also important that individuals and the department as a whole are prepared to tolerate mistakes as these will often be made in the early days of learning a new task.

On the job training is most appropriate for the learning of specific and not too complex tasks such as the preparation of the bank reconciliation or inputting of data into the computer.

HOW IT WORKS

One of Liz Spence's weekly tasks is the preparation of cost variances. Although she has some experience as a cost accountant she has never been required to prepare cost variances before. Ned has been preparing the weekly cost variances for the last 18 months and he is asked by John to help Liz with this new task.

Ned explains the information that is required, and the format in which the variance information must be produced. He then shows Liz how to produce the variances for four of the materials costs. After this he leaves her to try to calculate the variances for the remaining materials costs. He is at his desk performing his own tasks throughout this time and is able to help Liz on each occasion where she does not know what to do. By the end of the day both Liz and Ned are fairly happy that Liz has mastered this task.

Training courses

TRAINING COURSES can either be internal courses or external courses but they will tend to be more formal than other methods of training.

Some larger organisations have their own training departments and will run internal training courses. In other cases organisations may bring in external suppliers to run the type of training course required. INTERNAL TRAINING COURSES may be most appropriate in a the following types of circumstances:

- as a basic introductory course if there are a large number of recruits at any one time of the year

- where there is new legislation or regulations which affect a number of employees who must all learn about the changes

- where a training need is identified amongst a number of employees, such as an improvement to customer relations being required, a specific course can be run for all the relevant employees.

EXTERNAL TRAINING COURSES are courses that are run outside the organisation. These are most appropriate in the following circumstances:

- where the organisation does not have the resources to run internal training courses ie it does not have a training function

- where individual employees require specific professional training such as for AAT or other professional qualifications.

Computer based training

COMPUTER BASED TRAINING is interactive training via a personal computer. There is a move towards many types of training, including professional qualification training, to be accessed in this manner. The employee can either take part in the training during working hours at set times or in their own time on a personal computer at home.

Mentoring

MENTORING is the use of specially trained individuals within the organisation to act as an advisor and a guide to employees in order to help them develop both personally and in their career. Usually the mentor will not be the employee's line manager or any other manager that he generally reports to. A mentor should be available for help and advice for all aspects of the employees life at work and in particular to help with problems that employees may face in their working life.

Activity 3

What would be the most appropriate method of training in each of the following circumstances?

(i)   An employee has recently qualified as an AAT Technician and wishes to move on to study for the CIMA qualification.

(ii)   Due to the imminence of 2005 it is necessary that all of the accounts personnel should be briefed regarding the importance of International Accounting Standards.

(iii) A new member of the accounts department is struggling with her basic word processing skills.

(iv)   One accounts assistant who generally works in the sales ledger department has recently had added to her role the responsibility for petty cash which had previously been the responsibility of the cashier.

Project note

For your project you should try to include evidence of your review of staff competencies and training needs together with details of the training actually arranged for employees.

CHAPTER OVERVIEW

- individual employees will have a variety of skills or competencies - these will include technical skills, professional knowledge, administrative skills, computer based skills and interpersonal skills

- a staff appraisal scheme is a method of formally assessing the competencies of individual employees and identifying areas for development and training

- the formal appraisal process includes the following stages - setting the critieria for assessment, writing the appraisal report, the appraisal interview, the assessment review, preparation of an action plan and the follow up process

- from a manager's perspective the appraisal interview has four main stages - preparation, the interview itself, the appraisal report and follow up procedures

- personal development plans will normally be set by individuals and should have the elements summarised by the mnemonic SMARTER

- training is an element of personal development where an individual's training needs are assessed and the appropriate method of training provided

- the main methods of training are induction training, on the job training, training courses, computer based training and mentoring

KEY WORDS

Staff competencies The technical skills, professional knowledge, administrative skills, computer based skills and interpersonal skills possessed by employees

Technical skills Techniques, processes and skills required to carry out an employee's tasks

Professional knowledge Knowledge of external legal and professional regulations required for an employee's job

Administrative skills Skills in the area of administration which are an adjunct of an employee's job

Computer based skills IT skills necessary to carry out an employee's job

Interpersonal skills The ways in which individuals behave with other individuals

Appraisal scheme A formal method of assessing the skills, competencies and training and development needs of employees

Appraisal report A formal report assessing the performance of the employee during the past period

Appraisal interview A forum for joint discussion of the appraisal report, agreement of areas for improvement, identification of training and development needs and agreement of future actions

Personal development The formulation of personal and career goals

Personal development plans An individual employee's plans for their personal and career future

CHAPTER OVERVIEW cont.

KEY WORDS

Training Teaching or coaching employees in the skills required to perform their jobs

Training needs Skills the employee needs to carry out his current job and to progress towards personal development goals

Induction training Initial training given to new employees when they first arrive in an organisation

On the job training Teaching or showing an employee the skills and techniques required to carry out his job

Training courses Formal, classroom based courses

Internal training courses Courses that are run within the organisation

External training courses Courses that are run outside the organisation

Computer based training Interactive training via a personal computer

Mentoring Guidance for an employee from a specially trained individual within the organisation

HOW MUCH HAVE YOU LEARNED?

1   Give six examples of technical skills that an accounts assistant might require.

2   Give three examples of professional knowledge that an accounts assistant might require.

3   What are the main objectives of a typical staff appraisal scheme?

4   Briefly explain the main stages of a typical staff appraisal scheme.

5   Briefly explain what is meant by setting SMARTER personal development plans.

6   What are training needs and how might they be identified for an individual employee?

7   What might be the most appropriate method of training in each of the following situations?

(i)   The finance director has decided that the accounts department requires general updating on the requirements of the Data Protection Act

(ii)   A new purchase ledger clerk has just joined the accounts department and has little idea of her role or how the department works

(iii)   One of the accounts assistants is struggling with double entry bookkeeping

(iv)   Another accounts assistant made it clear at his recent appraisal that he would like to start studying for the AAT qualification.

chapter 5:
CONTINGENCY PLANS

chapter coverage

However well planned a department or project team is there is always the possibility that things might go wrong. A well organised manager will have contingency plans in place for possible major problems and in this chapter we will consider those contingency plans. The guidance for Unit 10 states that students need to show that they prepare contingency plans to cover a variety of problems that can reduce the likelihood of objectives, targets and deadlines being met.

The topics that we shall cover are:

✍ contingencies

✍ contingency plans

✍ computer risks

✍ staff absences

✍ changes in work patterns and demands

KNOWLEDGE AND UNDERSTANDING AND PERFORMANCE CRITERIA COVERAGE

Performance criteria – Element 10.1

C   Prepare in collaboration with management contingency plans to meet possible emergencies

F   Co-ordinate work activities effectively and in accordance with work plans and contingencies plans

CONTINGENCIES

Before we look at contingency plans we will firstly consider what contingencies are. A CONTINGENCY is effectively a risk of something that may or may not happen. An organisation will face a variety of risks to its operations and to its accounting function and, as we will see in the next chapter, there will be controls built into the operations and functions of the organisation to counter these risks. However controls against risks will only be built into a system if the benefits of the controls outweigh the costs.

In some cases the management of the organisation will take the view that the risk will be run, as the cost of guarding against it is too great.

HOW IT WORKS

Within Angus Bell Ltd, as with many organisations, there is a risk that if a purchase invoice is received from a supplier then it will automatically be paid even if the goods have never been received and indeed if the supplier is not even genuine.

This is a fairly common risk and will be one that is guarded against by a simple system of ensuring that all purchase invoices are checked not only to the original purchase order to ensure that the goods were ordered from this supplier, but also to the goods received note to ensure that they were actually received. If all of the checks are valid then the invoice will be paid. This is an example of a control within the accounting system.

However there is also a risk that the entire accounting staff might be affected by food poisoning after a night out together. This is the type of risk that although it exists may not necessarily be worth guarding against by any system of control such as paying a retainer to a temporary recruitment agency to ensure that the accounts department can be staffed at short notice at any time. The cost of the control may be too great given the likelihood of the risk arising but this will be a management decision.

Contingency plans

In the example of Angus Bell Ltd above, although there will be no control over the risk of large scale absence in the accounts department there should be a CONTINGENCY PLAN in place just in case this does happen.

Contingency plans are therefore plans of how to deal with risks that are recognised but by their very nature are unlikely although possible.

Contingency planning

CONTINGENCY PLANNING will involve assessing unplanned events which may occur from time to time. The assessment will involve determining the following:

- the probability of the event happening

- the level of impact of the event on the business

If there is a reasonable probability of the event happening and the effect on the business would be material then a contingency plan should normally be considered.

HOW IT WORKS

The risk of the building which Angus Bell Ltd operates in collapsing is remote although the effect on the business would be major.

The probability of the accounts department running out of coffee is probably reasonably high on occasions but the effect on the business is minimal.

In neither of these cases would it be worth having a contingency plan.

However the chance of a computer break down due to a power cut might be viewed as both reasonably probable and likely to have a significant effect on the accounting function. This is the type of situation where a contingency plan should be in operation.

Identifying risks

As you will discover in the next chapter, many of the risks faced by an organisation will be dealt with by a system of internal control. However one of the jobs of a manager is to identify other potential risks that must be considered and planned for. This should be a continuous process and should include the following:

- consider problems that the accounting department has had in the past

- communicate with the staff in the accounting department as they may be aware   of potential problems that you as a manager are not aware of

- keep up to date with all aspects of the accounting department's work and try to anticipate problems that might occur.

Possible risks

The main possible emergencies that we will be considering for Unit 10 are the following:

- computer systems not being fully functional

- staff absences

- changes in work patterns and demands

In the rest of the chapter we shall consider how managers can assess the impact of these possible events on the business and the plans they can make to deal with these types of risks and problems.

Activity 1

Define what is meant by contingency planning.

COMPUTER PROBLEMS

As most organisations, and accounting functions in particular, become more and more computerised there are of course more and more risks of malfunction and loss of information from problems with the computer system. There are a large number of events that may cause a failure of the computer system. Such events may cause a partial failure of just a part of the computer system or a total failure affecting all parts of the system.

Some computer risks should be dealt with by computer controls as a matter of course. These will include:

- passwords

- anti-virus controls

- backup procedures

Passwords

In order to try to minimise the risk of unauthorised access to the computer system or parts of it and therefore the deliberate corruption of software or hardware most organisations will have a system of PASSWORDS. A password is a unique code for each individual computer user which allows them access to the system. The password system should keep unauthorised users out of the system but to be effective the following controls should be exercised over passwords:

- they should be confidential
- they should be kept hidden
- they should be changed regularly
- they should not be obvious.

Some passwords will allow users into only part of the computer system for example access to the sales ledger but not to the payroll system.

Viruses

A VIRUS is a computer program that can infect a computer causing data and files to be corrupted or destroyed.

Controls against viruses should be standard practice in all computerised environments and should include the following:

- anti-virus software which will detect and eradicate most viruses before they have a chance to cause any damage

- internal rules regarding the opening of e-mail attachments

- internal rules regarding the downloading of disks which must be checked for viruses before being downloaded

- internal rules regarding the use of unauthorised software in the system.

Backup procedures

All computerised environments should have strict backup procedures which ensure that data input into the computer is regularly backed up and saved. It is important that all data and programs can be recreated if the original is lost.

Reasons for partial or total system failure

Despite the normal control procedures which cover the general risks of operating in a computer environment there are other reasons why it is possible that there may be a partial or total system failure. These may include:

- hardware faults

- loss of data due a system crash

- loss of data due to a power cut

- corruption of data or programs from either viruses not detected or from malicious individuals within or outside the organisation.

Possible contingency plans

Although these possibilities may seem fairly remote if they are viewed to have a reasonable probability of taking place contingency plans must be made to deal with them.

- if there is a hardware fault then even with backup data the fault must be diagnosed and corrected before any backup data can be used in the system. The organisation should ensure that it has a maintenance contract with the supplier who can deal with the fault and put it right.

- if data is lost due to a system crash or power cut regular backup of data will ensure the minimum of losses. However any data that has been lost must be re-input and processed as soon as the fault is dealt with or the power restored. This may mean that overtime has to be worked by all personnel in the accounting function in order to catch up for time lost.

- if one part of a system of the computer is corrupted or lost then the remaining computerised elements may continue as normal and all staff must help in reinstating the lost data for that part of the system or take over the normal roles of the employees in that part of the system whilst they reinstate the lost data

- an agreement with a computer bureau can ensure that its own systems are made available in the event of such an emergency.

Activity 2

If password control is to be effective within a computerised system what controls must be exercised?

STAFF ABSENCES

In all organisations there will obviously be occasions when staff are absent. Some absences will be short term whilst others will be longer term. Some absences can be planned for in advance whereas others cannot be predicted.

Short term absences

Short term absences will include:

- sickness
- holidays
- compassionate leave

Longer term absences

Longer term absences will include:

- study leave
- maternity leave

Predictable absences

Some types of staff absence, both short term and longer term, can be planned for as part of the normal procedures of the organisation.

Holidays - staff holidays will need to be booked in advance with the personnel manager or line manager and in a small department it may well be company policy that there is a maximum number of people who may be allowed to take holiday at any one time.

Study leave - if members of the accounts team are studying for professional exams such as the AAT qualification then there are likely to be occasions where they may need to take a number of weeks off to attend revision courses and sit exams or assessments. Such study leave should be known about well in advance by the line manager. In many organisations it can be arranged that the student's duties can be covered by other members of the accounts department in their absence. If this is not possible then consideration should be given to recruitment of a temporary replacement for this period.

Maternity leave - maternity leave can be for a considerable number of months and therefore it may not be possible to expect other members of the accounts team to cover an employee's work for this period of time. Therefore recruitment of a temporary replacement may be necessary.

Unpredictable absence

Some staff absences cannot be predicted in advance and therefore arrangements cannot be made to deal with them in advance. Instead the absence must be dealt with as part of normal procedures or in more drastic cases there should be a contingency plan in place.

Staff sickness

From time to time it is obvious that members of staff will be off sick. In most cases this should not cause major disruption. If only one or two members of the accounts team are off sick for just a few days then their work can be dealt with as follows:

- urgent tasks can be done by other members of the accounts team
- non-urgent tasks can be caught up on when the staff member returns from sick leave.

Multi skilled employees

On a number of occasions in this section of the chapter we have mentioned that the work of an absent member of staff could be done by other members of staff in their absence. However this is only possible in either a large accounting department or in a department where the employees are multi skilled.

In a large accounting department it is likely that there will be more than one person carrying out the same jobs. For example in a large sales ledger section there may be five accounts assistant who deal with input of invoices to the sales ledger, matching of payments from debtors and preparation of monthly statements. If one of these accounts assistants is off sick then in the short term their urgent tasks can be covered by the other four accounts assistants who do the same job.

However in many smaller accounting functions there are a limited number of staff who each have their own specialist functions. Therefore if one member of staff is away on sick leave there may be no one else who is capable of doing their job. This is where JOB ROTATION and the resultant MULTI SKILLED EMPLOYEES come in to play. Both of these were mentioned in an earlier chapter but we shall put them into context again here. If employees have experience of doing not only their own specialist job in the department but also some experience of other jobs in the accounting function then it is easier to cover important work when someone is absent.

HOW IT WORKS

Given below is the departmental structure for the accounting function of Angus Bell Ltd which you have come across before in this Course Companion.

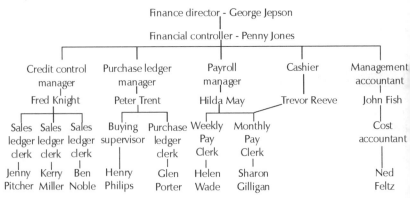

Within the credit control function all three sales ledger clerks are capable of carrying out all sales ledger roles although in normal circumstances they each have their own individual specialist roles.

Both the weekly and monthly pay clerks are capable of dealing with weekly and monthly payrolls although this would require additional assistance from the payroll supervisor.

The cost accountant, Ned Feltz, has spent some time dealing with writing up the cash book and petty cash book and also with the purchase ledger system. Glen Porter, although currently the purchase ledger clerk, spent some time dealing with cost accounts at his previous organisation.

Within this department therefore, due to the multi skills of the employees, most short term staff absences could be covered by other members of the accounting function.

Activity 3

What is meant by multi skilled employees and what advantages do they have?

Situations where contingency planning is required

As we have seen so far in this section most staff absences can be planned for in advance or dealt with by other members of the accounting function. However there are certain situations that may need to be considered and a contingency plan drawn up:

- where a large number of the accounting function are off sick at any one time, eg when a flu bug hits the accounting department or a case of food poisoning from the same source

- where only a small number of staff are off sick but at a critical period such as the month end or more importantly at the half year or year end

- where staff are unable to come into work for other emergency reasons such as a gas leak in the building or a transport strike.

Internal contingency plan

One method of dealing with any of the events described above, or anything similar, is to deal with the situation internally within the organisation. Contingency plans could include the following:

- reschedule work so that all non-urgent work is delayed

- critically examine the tasks that are to be carried out and ensure that only truly essential tasks for the job in hand ie the half year financial statements, are actually carried out

- require the staff that are available to work significant amounts of overtime

- allocate work to other members of the team even if they are more senior and would not normally carry out such tasks

- seek help from other departments

External contingency plans

In the cases of staff absence where the situation cannot be dealt with internally, the recruitment of temporary staff must be considered. The organisation may wish to have an agreement with a recruitment agency that can be called upon at short notice in such emergency situations.

CHANGES IN WORK PATTERNS AND DEMAND

In general the work load of the accounting function should be fairly predictable. There will of course be times where there is more work than at other times, for example at the month end when the payroll is due, the monthly customer statements must be sent out and the monthly management accounts prepared. Again these increases in workload at these times can be predicted and plans made for overtime to be worked.

Preparation of financial accounts

A further obvious example of increase of work load is at the half year and year end where not only management accounts will be due but also financial accounts as well. At the year end in particular the financial statements for the year must be drafted and to make matters worse the auditors are also likely to require significant amounts of staff time.

The manager can plan for this by creating an expectation of increased amounts of overtime at this period or in extreme circumstances the manager could recruit temporary staff to cover routine work whilst the permanent staff deal with the year end routines and the preparation of the financial statements.

Increase in workload

If the general activities of the organisation increase this is likely to have a similar effect on the work load of the accounting function. The reason for the general increase in activity should have been predicted, additional products, upturn in the economy etc, and therefore the effect on the accounting function should also have been predicted. Once an increase in workload is predicted then recruitment should be considered - permanent staff if the increase is expected to be permanent, but only temporary staff if the increase is only of a temporary nature.

In a situation where there is an increase in workload in the accounting function additional staff may not be the only answer. A new and more efficient computer system may be the answer to dealing with the increased workload.

Decrease in workload

If there is a down turn in general activity levels, leading to less work for the accounting function, or the introduction of a new computer system requiring fewer man hours, the following steps might be considered:

- overtime ban
- voluntary redundancies
- part time working
- job sharing

Project note

For your project you should be showing evidence of 'contingency planning, in collaboration with management, for possible emergencies'. In many cases you will not have been involved in such contingency planning but having worked through this chapter you may consider that there are areas within your department or section which require a contingency plan which is not yet in existence, and you could build this into your project report.

CHAPTER OVERVIEW

- a contingency is an event or risk which may or may not happen - a contingency plan is a plan which is in operation in case such an event happens

- contingency planning involves assessing the probability of the event happening and the impact of that event on the business

- if there is a reasonable probability of the event happening and the effect on the business would be material then a contingency plan should normally be put in place

- a manager should be responsible for identifying possible risks to his department or section

- within a computerised accounting system there are a number of risks which may lead to partial or total system failure

- many of the risks within a computerised system are dealt with by computer controls such as passwords, virus protection and backup procedures

- other risks include hardware faults, loss of data due to a system crash or power failure or deliberate corruption of data, and contingency plans must be put into place

- in many cases the absence of staff will either be short term (and therefore manageable) or predictable but in some cases there will either be unpredictable absences or large scale absences which could disrupt the activities of the accounting function

- many staff absences can be dealt with by rescheduling of activities particularly if the accounts personnel are multi skilled - however at critical times of the year or where there are large numbers of absentees the effects may be more major and a contingency plan should be in place

- most changes in work patterns and demand for the accounting function's services should be fairly predictable and therefore can be planned in advance. However there may need to be contingency plans in place for additional recruitment in a time of expansion or overtime bans, voluntary redundancy, part time working or job sharing if the workload of the accounting function contracts

KEY WORDS

Contingency A risk which may or may not happen

Contingency plan A plan of how to deal with a risk that is recognised but by its nature is possible although unlikely

Contingency planning A method of assessing the probability of an unlikely event happening and the level of impact that this event would have on the business

Passwords A unique code which allows each individual access to the computer system

Virus A computer program that can infect a computer causing data and files to be corrupted or destroyed

Job rotation The practice of employees carrying out each others jobs on a rotating basis as well as their own specialist job

Multi skilled employees Employees who can perform more than one task within their department or section

HOW MUCH HAVE YOU LEARNED?

1   Explain what is meant by the following terms:

   (i)   a contingency

   (ii)   a contingency plan

   (iii) contingency planning

2   Explain how the probability of an event occurring and its likely effect on the business affect contingency planning.

3   How might a manager of an accounts department identify risks to his department that are not covered by internal accounting controls?

4   How might a business attempt to limit the risk of viruses in its computer system?

5   Briefly explain three possible contingency plans for a partial or total computer system failure.

6   In what situations might contingency plans be required for staff absences?

chapter 6:
IMPROVEMENTS TO THE ACCOUNTING SYSTEM

chapter coverage 📖

In this chapter we will start to consider Element 10.2 of Unit 10. This element is concerned with identifying weaknesses in an accounting system and making recommendations to rectify these. You will be required to make recommendations to rectify weaknesses and to consider the impact that these would have on the organisation. You are also required to update the accounting system to comply with both internal and external factors such as changes in organisational structure or changes in legislation or accounting standards, and to subsequently check that the post-change output is correct.

The topics that we shall cover are:

- ✎ internal control systems
- ✎ types of internal controls
- ✎ internal checks
- ✎ SWOT analysis and the accounting system
- ✎ quality
- ✎ efficiency
- ✎ cost-effectiveness
- ✎ recommendations for improvements
- ✎ updating the system
- ✎ PEST analysis

knowledge and understanding – the business environment

■   external regulations affecting accounting practices

knowledge and understanding – methods of measuring cost effectiveness

■   Methods of measuring cost-effectiveness
■   Techniques for influencing and negotiating with decision makers and resource holders

Performance criteria – Element 10.2

A   Weaknesses and potential for improvements to the accounting system are identified and considered for their impact on the operation of the organisation

C   Methods of operating are regularly reviewed in respect of their cost-effectiveness, reliability and speed

D   Recommendations are made to the appropriate people in a clear, easily understood format

E   Recommendations are supported by a clear rationale which includes an explanation of any assumptions made

F   The system is updated in accordance with changes that affect the way the system should operate. Such updates are subsequently checked to ensure that the required results have been achieved

INTERNAL CONTROL SYSTEMS

In this chapter we are considering Element 10.2, 'Identify opportunities to improve the effectiveness of an accounting system'. The types of improvement that we might be considering could relate to controls within the accounting system, the cost-effectiveness of the accounting system, the quality of the accounting system and its reliability and speed. Therefore we shall start the chapter by considering the internal control system which will be in operation to some degree or another within an accounting system.

Aims of an internal control system

An INTERNAL CONTROL SYSTEM can be defined as 'the whole system of controls, financial and otherwise, established by the management in order to carry on the business of the enterprise in an orderly and efficient manner, ensure adherence to management policies, safeguard the assets and secure as far as possible the completeness and accuracy of the records'.

Therefore the aims of such a system of internal control are as follows:

- efficiency of the operations
- adherence to management policies
- safeguard the assets of the business
- ensure completeness and accuracy of the accounting records

The system of internal control is not one which just relates to the accounting function of the business but to all elements of management control such as quality of output of production or controls over late arrival of employees.

Activity 1

What are the four main aims of an internal control system?

Internal controls

Within the internal control system the individual components are known as INTERNAL CONTROLS.

There are two main types of internal control:

- administrative controls
- accounting controls

ADMINISTRATIVE CONTROLS are the methods and procedures in the business which are concerned with the operational efficiency of the business and adherence to management policies.

ACCOUNTING CONTROLS are the methods and procedures that are concerned with safeguarding the assets of the business and ensuring the completeness, accuracy and reliability of the financial records.

TYPES OF INTERNAL CONTROLS

There are eight types of internal control which can be remembered using the mnemonic SPAM SOAP.

Segregation of duties
Physical
Authorisation and approval
Management

Supervision
Organisation
Arithmetical and accounting
Personnel

We will now consider each of the these general types of internal control in turn.

Segregation of duties

SEGREGATION OF DUTIES is a key internal control whereby wherever possible the aim is to ensure that one individual cannot record and process a complete transaction. By appropriate segregation of duties the risk of intentional manipulation or error is reduced. Wherever possible the following functions should be carried out by different personnel:

- authorisation
- execution
- custody
- recording
- systems development and daily operations

HOW IT WORKS

Given below is the organisation structure of the accounts department of Angus Bell Ltd as we will be using it throughout this chapter.

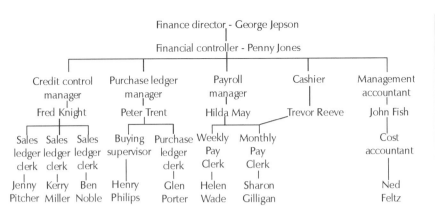

In the morning Helen Wade opens the post and makes a list of cheques received which she totals and passes to Trevor Reeve for recording in the cash received book. Later in the day Ned Feltz takes the cheques to the bank to pay them in.

This is an example of segregation of duties as different people have the following duties:

- initial recording of the receipts
- entering into the accounting records
- paying into the bank

Physical control

This is a straightforward security control whereby access to the assets of the business are restricted to authorised personnel only. This will often be by the use of locks, safes etc for physical assets and passwords for computer information.

HOW IT WORKS

In the accounts department of Angus Bell Ltd Sharon Gilligan deals with the petty cash. The petty cash box is kept in a locked cupboard in Trevor Reeve's office and the box is always locked when Sharon is not using it. Only Trevor and Sharon have keys to the box and the cupboard.

Authorisation and approval

All transactions should be authorised or approved by an appropriate responsible person within the organisation. In most cases there should be authorisation limits set.

HOW IT WORKS

In Angus Bell Ltd, Peter Trent, the purchase ledger manager, can authorise payments to suppliers upto £5,000 but any amounts above this must be authorised for payment by Penny Jones, the financial controller.

Management controls

Management controls are any controls exercised by managers outside the day-to-day routine. Such controls will include the following:

- supervisory controls
- internal audit
- review of management accounts
- comparison of actual results to budget
- other special review procedures

Not all companies are large enough for an internal audit department. However where there is an INTERNAL AUDIT function its role is twofold:

- operational audits - the purpose of which are to monitor management performance at all levels and to ensure that the business is operating to the degree of efficiency required

- systems audits - testing and evaluation of the internal controls of the organisation.

The two most important features of the internal audit function are:

- it is directly accountable to the highest levels of management and often the audit committee of the Board of Directors

- it is and is seen to be independent of all levels of management.

Supervisory controls

The operation and recording of day to day transactions should be supervised by a responsible official.

Organisational controls

In order for transactions and recording of those transactions to be adequately controlled it is important that all employees understand the organisational structure and in particular the lines of authority and responsibility. The responsibility and reporting structure of the organisation should be quite clear to all employees.

HOW IT WORKS

In the accounts department of Angus Bell Ltd you may remember that Sharon Gilligan is not just the monthly pay clerk but is also responsible for the petty cash system. As such she reports to both Hilda May, the payroll supervisor, and to Trevor Reeve, the cashier. For this system to work properly all three employees must be aware of this authority and responsibility structure.

Arithmetical and accounting controls

These are controls within the accounting system which ensure that all transactions are:

- authorised
- complete
- correctly recorded
- accurately processed

Such controls will include the following:

- control totals
- checking arithmetical accuracy of records and data input
- reconciliations
- control accounts
- trial balances

HOW IT WORKS

In Angus Bell Ltd at the end of each month the following reconciliations are performed:

- sales ledger control account reconciliation
- purchase ledger control account reconciliation
- bank reconciliation

Personnel controls

Personnel controls are methods and procedures to ensure that those carrying out duties within the organisation are capable and competent to carry out those responsibilities. This covers recruitment, selection, qualifications and training as well as the interpersonal skills and innate personalities of employees.

How to set up an internal control system

With the SPAM SOAP internal controls in mind the management of a organisation will select the most appropriate controls for their organisation This may not include all of the controls listed above - for example a sma organisation will normally struggle to have adequate segregation of dutie However once the controls have been implemented they will then form th internal control system of the organisation.

Project note

For your project you should review the internal controls in your department or section and consider whether it is possible to improve those controls in any way

Activity 2

What are the eight general controls summarised in the mnemonic SPAM SOAP?

Internal checks

INTERNAL CHECKS are part of a system of internal control but have a muc more restricted meaning. Internal checks are checks on the day-to-da transactions which are part of the routine system where the work of on person is independently checked by another or is complementary to th work of another.

Internal checks are an important part of the accounting system and ar designed to prevent or to detect at an early stage any errors or fraud. Man of these checks will be arithmetical checks on the accuracy of processing c transactions using pre-lists, post-lists and various control totals.

A PRE-LIST is a list of document totals which is drawn up before th transactions are processed. A POST-LIST is a list of transactions drawn u during or after the processing. A CONTROL TOTAL is simply a total of number of documents or transactions which is used for a control purpose b comparing it with another total which should be the same. Batch totals ar examples of control totals that are used widely within a computerise accounting system.

HOW IT WORKS

As we saw earlier in the chapter, when the post arrives in the morning Helen Wade opens it and lists and totals any cheques received. The cheques and the list are then passed to Trevor Reeve to enter into the cash received book. The total of the cheque list can then be compared to the total receipts recorded in the cash received book.

Purpose of internal checks

The main purposes of internal checks are:

- to break down procedures into separate steps

- to segregate tasks so that responsibility for a task or transaction can be traced to an individual

- to keep the records of control totals etc as evidence of the accuracy of the accounting

- to reduce the possibility of fraud or error

Limitations of internal controls

An effective internal control system is necessary for all organisations but however good the system is it cannot necessarily guarantee total efficiency and completeness and accuracy of the accounting records. The system is only as good as the way in which it is operated. There are limitations to the internal control system, such as:

- collusion of two or more employees can defeat the aims of segregation of duties and facilitate fraudulent activities (this will be dealt with in more detail in the next chapter)

- authorisation controls are only effective if not abused by the person in authority

- even though managers have set up the controls they can also override them for their own purposes.

Project note

As well as reviewing the actual internal controls in operation in your section of the organisation, consider as well how effective these internal controls and internal checks are in practice.

SWOT ANALYSIS

SWOT ANALYSIS is a method that can be used to carry out a situation analysis of an accounting system in order to find evidence for potential improvements in it. SWOT stands for:

Strengths
Weaknesses
Opportunities
Threats

Strengths and weaknesses will be internal good and bad points about the workings of the accounting system. Opportunities and threats will tend to be external factors that may affect the accounting system.

Strengths will generally be areas of the accounting system where the control system is strong and internal checks are working well. Opportunities will be areas where the accounting system can perhaps be changed to take advantage of external changes in circumstance. Weaknesses will be areas where the internal controls are either non-existent or not working as they should. Threats are areas of weakness which could cause problems due to external factors. Both weaknesses and threats are areas where there is likely to be a potential for fraud or error within the accounting system (covered in more detail in the next chapter).

Each area of strength, weakness, opportunity or threat can then be graded as high, medium or low importance in order to conclude about any possible improvements in the accounting system.

HOW IT WORKS

As we have seen, the procedure for cheques received in the post at Angus Bell Ltd is that they are listed by Helen Wade, entered into the cash received book by Trevor Reeve and paid into the bank by Ned Feltz. A monthly bank reconciliation is prepared by Trevor Reeve.

The credit control manager, Fred Knight, has just discovered that the two main competitors to Angus Bell Ltd have recently introduced a settlement discount system for some of their credit customers.

In the purchase ledger section of the accounts department, Henry Philips checks all purchase invoices received to the related purchase order. However the related goods received notes remain with the stores department.

Helen Wade, the weekly pay clerk, pays 26 of the 100 weekly paid employees in cash whereas the rest are paid through the BACS system.

If a SWOT analysis were to be carried out using this information about elements of the accounting system the following conclusions would be likely to be drawn:

Strengths

- segregation of duties for cash receipts
- monthly bank reconciliation as accounting control

Weaknesses

- purchase invoices and orders are not compared to goods received notes

- some weekly paid employees are still paid in cash which increases the administrative burden and the risk of fraud

Opportunities

- the fact that two major competitors have started to offer settlement discounts might open the way for Angus Bell Ltd to follow suit and improve the company's cash flow

Threats

- there is an increased risk of fraud or theft when paying wages in cash

- the offering of the settlement discount by the competitors might be seen as a threat if Angus Bell Ltd did not also start to offer discounts as the company may lose some business to the competitors

Activity 3

What are the four elements of a SWOT analysis? Give an example of each in the context of an accounting system.

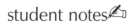

METHODS OF OPERATION IN THE ACCOUNTING SYSTEM

Element 10.2 is not just concerned with potential improvements to the accounting system but also with the methods of operation in the accounting system and its effectiveness. Performance criteria 10.2 C states that 'methods of operating are regularly reviewed in respect of their cost-effectiveness, reliability and speed'. Therefore in this section of the chapter we will consider other aspects of the accounting system and in particular:

- quality
- efficiency
- cost-effectiveness

QUALITY

QUALITY could be described as the 'degree of excellence of the product or service' or 'how well the product or service serves its purpose'.

Quality therefore requires care by the provider of the product or service but is actually judged by the customer or the receiver of the product or service. The product or service will only be perceived as having quality if it satisfies that customer. Therefore the product or service must have two main elements if it is to satisfy the customer:

- it must be fit for the purpose for which it has been acquired
- it must represent value for money to the customer.

This does not mean that products or services need to be made more expensive by using better materials or more highly skilled staff. Provided that the product or service does what it is meant to do and is viewed as value for money to the customer then this product or service will have quality.

Customers

Key to the definition and understanding of quality is the perception of the customer. Here we need to consider the customer from the perspective of the accounting function. The accounting function will be providing services both internally and externally and can therefore be said to have both INTERNAL CUSTOMERS and EXTERNAL CUSTOMERS.

nternal customers are any other parts of the business for which the accounting department may provide a service. This will include the following:

- employees who are paid by the payroll section
- employees claiming petty cash refunds
- line managers requiring reports and management information
- senior management requiring reports and management information
- other sections such as stores or sales requiring information from the accounting function

External customers are those outside the organisation for whom the accounting department provides information including:

- customers being invoiced and sent statements

- credit suppliers being paid

- shareholders requiring annual financial statements

- banks or other lenders requiring management accounts or financial forecasts.

The importance of customers

Although the accounting function does not provide a product as such to its customers, its treatment of its customers is still important. The accounts department provides a service to its external customers in the provision of information such as invoices and monthly statements for debtors. It is important that the information provided is correct, for example if a credit customer is constantly having to ring up to say that their invoices are incorrect or the balance on their statement is not what is due then they may well consider taking their business elsewhere.

Whenever information is provided to another function of the business we see the accounts department dealing with an internal customer. Although the internal customer may not have a choice about whether or not to use the accounts department in order to efficiently and effectively reach organisational goals and targets, it is important that the information provided by the accounting function is of the required quality.

Getting it right first time

One of the key principles of quality is the concept of GETTING IT RIGHT FIRST TIME. The concept is that the most efficient and cost-effective method of operating is to get the job right the first time that it is done and then to 'get more right next time'. Therefore there is a continuous cycle of improvement in the service provided.

student notes✍

Managing quality

As a manager in the accounting function your concern will be with the quality of the service provided to both internal and external customers. Managing this quality is an element of the system of control and will have the following stages:

Stage 1 Set quality standards for each area of the accounting function

Stage 2 Establish procedures and methods of operation to ensure that these quality standards are met

Stage 3 Monitor the actual quality of the service

Stage 4 Take steps to improve the methods of operating to ensure that the quality standards are met

HOW IT WORKS

The financial controller of Angus Bell Ltd, Penny Jones, has set a target to the credit control department that invoices should generally be sent out to customers on the day that the goods are delivered. However recognising that this is not always possible the target to be met is that 90% of invoices are sent out within two days of delivery and the remaining 10% within four days of delivery.

Ben Noble largely deals with the preparation and sending out of invoices each day but if he feels that the target cannot be met due to other commitments he approaches Fred Knight who will authorise one of the other sales ledger clerks to help him with this task.

Once a month Penny Jones will carry out a test by comparing delivery notes to invoices to check that this target is being met.

Project note

As a manager in the accounting function, or by observing managers and operations in the accounting function, you should assess whether there are any improvements to the quality of the output of the department or section which you could recommend and include in your report.

Activity 4

Give three examples of quality within an accounting system.

EFFICIENCY

EFFICIENCY can be described as a means of getting the most output for a given level of input. This may be fairly easy to visualise for a production department such as a factory but harder in the context of an accounting function. However you may wish to consider the methods of operation within the function that you manage, or are observing being managed, and determine whether these operations are being carried out as efficiently as possible.

One means of raising the efficiency of the operations is to study what is being done currently and recommend any re-organisations that may lead to the operations being carried out more efficiently. This is technically known as WORK STUDY which will normally be carried out by a specialist, but the principles behind work study can be used within a management capacity to observe the operations and consider the need for any improvements.

Project note

Your observations may lead to recommendations to improve procedures, methods or systems, communication, controls and possibly the organisation structure in the department.

Assessing efficiency

There are five main steps in assessing efficiency - these are five sets of questions that can be asked about each of the operations that take place in the accounting function.

Step 1 - what?
What is the purpose of the operation?
What is being done and why?
What else could or should be done?

Step 2 - where?
Where is it being done?
Why is it being done there?
Where else could or should it be done?

Step 3 - when?
When is it done?
Why is it done then?
When else could or should it be done?

Step 4 - who?
Who does it?
Why does that person do it?
Who else could or should do it?

Step 5 - how?
How is it done?
Why is it done that way?
How else could or should it be done?

Ask these questions in the order listed and this should enable a manager to assess the efficiency of that particular operation and to consider recommending improvements to the efficiency.

HOW IT WORKS

Fred Knight has been reviewing the operations of his sales ledger clerk during the annual appraisal interviews. He has discovered the following:

- Jenny Pitcher prints out the individual debtor accounts from the sales ledger at the end of each month for the preparation of the sales ledger control account reconciliation

- Kerry Noble prints out the individual debtor accounts from the sales ledger at the end of each month for use in the preparation of the bad debts listing

- Ben Noble also prints out the individual debtor accounts from the sales ledger at the end of each month in order to prepare the customer statements for the month.

Clearly all three sales ledger clerks are carrying out the same task for different purposes. Fred Knight decides that from now on Kerry Noble will print out three copies of the debtor accounts at each month end for use by all three sales ledger clerks.

Activity 5

What is meant by efficiency?

COST-EFFECTIVENESS

EFFECTIVENESS can be described as the means of achieving the desired objective. COST-EFFECTIVENESS is achieving that objective at the minimum cost level. The work of the accounting function should be carried out at the required quality level in order to meet the department's objectives but at the lowest possible cost.

One of the roles of a manager or supervisor will be to control costs and possibly even to cut the costs incurred by their department or section.

Budgets and control

The accounts department, in common with all other areas of the business, will normally have a budget set for it at the start of the period. The manager or supervisor may or may not have been involved in the setting of this budget but he will be concerned with ensuring that the costs of the department stay within the budgeted figures. The budgetary control system will work as follows:

- budget is set for department or section

- manager must compare actual costs to budgeted costs - the difference between these are known as VARIANCES

- the manager must investigate the causes of any significant variances and take any necessary action to resolve the problems that have caused the variance

- the cause of the variance and any necessary action will normally be reported to a higher level of management

Types of cost in an accounting environment

The types of cost that will be incurred in an accounting department are normally as follows:

- labour costs - this will be the major cost of the department and will consist of the basic pay and overtime pay for permanent employees and the costs of any temporary employees

- stationery used in the department

- overheads such as heat, light, power and rent

- equipment and computer costs

Controllable and non-controllable costs

CONTROLLABLE COSTS are those over which the manager responsible has some control and can influence the amount of the cost incurred. NON-CONTROLLABLE COSTS are other costs incurred by the department or section over which the manager has no control.

In your position as a manager or supervisor in an accounts department or section you will find that your department incurs both controllable and non-controllable costs.

Permanent labour costs

The cost of the basic pay of the permanent employees is not normally controllable as they will be paid for the hours that they are contracted to work. However overtime payments to employees are a controllable cost. The manager should aim to schedule work in order to incur the minimum necessary overtime hours.

Temporary labour costs

We saw in an earlier chapter how it might be necessary to employ temporary staff at times when the workload of the department is too great to be handled by the permanent employees or due to a major disruption such as the surprise resignation of a number of accounts staff at any one time. However the manager or supervisor should try to schedule the work of the department to ensure that the minimum of temporary labour is required.

Stationery costs

Direct costs such as the stationery used in the department are directly controllable by the manager or supervisor. As part of the checks on the efficiency of operations the manager should ensure that there is no unnecessary form filling and no wastage of stationery.

Overheads

Some overheads such as heat, light and power costs will be controllable by the manager or supervisor by ensuring that heating, lights and equipment are turned off at night. However other overhead costs such as rent are likely to be non-controllable. If the accounts department is part of a larger building the rent will be negotiated by senior management and then a portion will be allocated as a cost of the accounting department. This is not a controllable cost of the accounts manager.

Efficiency of operations

As we saw earlier, as a manager you may need to review the efficiency of the operations of the accounting function and this can have a direct impact on the costs of the department. If an operation such as payment of supplier invoices can be achieved to the same level of efficiency and quality but in less time this may lead to less overtime being worked and therefore reduction in departmental costs.

HOW IT WORKS

Returning to Angus Bell Ltd - in the previous example Fred Knight discovered a duplication of duties regarding the printing of debtor accounts at the month end. By using only one sales ledger clerk for this task the other two are freed up to carry out their other tasks and this may well reduce any overtime worked and its associated costs particularly as this takes place at the month end when all of the accounts staff are busier than normal.

Project note

For your project you may be able to identify ways in which the cost-effectiveness of your department or section can be improved. However as well as identifying such efficiencies you will also need to be able to make clear, well argued recommendations as to how such improvements can be introduced.

Activity 6

What is meant by cost-effectiveness?

RECOMMENDATIONS FOR IMPROVEMENTS

So far in this chapter we have considered a variety of elements of the accounting system:

- the internal control system
- the quality of output
- the efficiency of the department
- the cost-effectiveness of the department

In any of these areas, as a manager or supervisor, you may be able to identify areas where improvements can be made.

Types of possible recommendations

Given below is a list of possible ideas for recommendations for improvements to the accounting system - this list is by no means exhaustive but it might give you some ideas:

- additional internal controls
- additional internal checks
- reorganisation of office layout

- rescheduling of tasks
- re-allocation of duties between staff members
- elimination or redesign of forms
- computerisation of manual operations

Once any such recommendations have been identified it will normally be the case that the manager or supervisor will not have the authority to carry through the changes without further authorisation. Therefore the recommendations must be made, either orally or in writing, to the appropriate person within the organisation.

Making recommendations

You may find that many people within an organisation are resistant to change. These may be the employees working for you in your department or section or the senior management to whom you report. Therefore any recommendations that you are to make must be clearly argued and effectively sold to both the managers who will have to authorise those changes and the staff who will have to implement and work with the changes.

Recommendations made to management

When making recommendations for changes to senior management you should ensure that your arguments are very clear.

- explain the current method of operation

- explain why this method is not working or why it is not as efficient or cost-effective as it could be

- explain how the method of operation could be changed to be more effective

- outline clearly any assumptions that you have made in coming to this conclusion

HOW IT WORKS

It was noted earlier that within the purchase ledger section goods received notes were not checked to purchase invoices and purchase orders before the purchase invoice was paid. Peter Trent, a fairly recent recruit as purchase ledger manager has noticed this and has written the following memo to Penny Jones, the financial controller.

MEMO

To: Penny Jones, Financial controller
From: Peter Trent, Purchase ledger manager
Date: 2 March 2004
Subject: Purchase invoice payments

I have noted that the current system for authorising purchase invoices for payment requires that the purchase invoice is matched to the related purchase order. This ensures that the goods being paid for are those that were indeed ordered.

However the purchase invoice and purchase order are not matched to the goods received note. This means that it is entirely possible that we may be paying for goods that were not actually received. The current system is that the goods received notes are kept in the stores department.

I recommend that a copy of each goods received note is sent to Henry Philips so that when purchase invoices are received he can check that the goods were not only ordered but were also in fact received.

This will of course increase Henry's workload but I will discuss this with him and determine a sensible solution by transferring some of Henry's other tasks to Glen Porter who is not currently overloaded with work.

Please let me know if you are happy for me to implement this change. If so can you please inform the stores department of the new policy of sending copies of each goods received note to Henry.

UPDATING THE SYSTEM

However good an accounting system is it will require updating on occasions for changes that are required either due to internal factors or external factors.

Internal factors that may affect the accounting system include changes in organisational structure or feedback from customers. External factors that might lead to changes in the accounting system could be changes in company law, VAT rates or Financial Reporting Standards.

Not only must the system be updated but then the updates must be checked to ensure that the results that are achieved are those that are required.

Internal factors affecting change

Once an accounting system has been set up then it should largely continue in the same manner for some considerable time. However if improvements are identified then there may be changes required to the system but also there may be factors that change within the organisation which require an update of the system.

The two internal factors mentioned in the Unit 10 Guidance notes are:

- changes in the organisational structure
- responses to customer surveys

Changes in organisational structure

The importance of organisational structure to the way in which a business i managed and in turn the way in which the accounting system works wa considered in Chapter 1. If the organisational structure changes then this wi inevitably change the reporting system of the accounting function and the methods of operation of the accounting system.

For example if the organisational structure is changed from one that i product based to one that is geographically based this will have a significan effect on the accounting function. In a product based organisationa structure, emphasis within the accounting function is on the reporting of cost per product and profitability per product. In a geographically base organisational structure the emphasis is on the costs and profitability of geographical unit.

Response to customer surveys

Earlier in this chapter we considered the quality of the output of th accounting function and in particular the concept of the accounting functio having customers. It was identified that one of the significant extern customers for the accounting function is that of customers and cred customers in particular. Many organisations, in particular servic organisations, spend a lot of time and money surveying their customers as what their needs and requirements are. This is all part of the provision quality.

The responses from customers may range from a request to be invoiced the end of each month, thereby improving their cash flow, to simple matte such as remittance advices being added to the end of statements sent out them. If the organisation is to provide a quality product and the accountir function is to provide a quality service such responses must be taken in consideration and the accounting systems will have to be changed accommodate these requirements.

External factors affecting change

In Chapter 1 we considered the external factors that affected accounti practices and these external factors may also cause changes in the accounti systems and methods of operation. It might be useful as a manager consider external factors in this context using a PEST ANALYSIS.

PEST analysis is a method of analysis which looks at factors that affect the accounting system from the following perspectives:

Political
Economic
Social
Technological

We will now consider how each of these in turn might affect the operations of the accounting system.

Political factors

There are a variety of political factors that can affect the operations of an accounting system. These might include the following:

- changes in NIC rates
- changes in VAT rates
- changes in company legislation regarding publication of financial statements
- changes in Financial Reporting Standards

Economic factors

Examples of economic factors that might affect the accounting system are:

- increase/decrease in volume of transactions due to general or specific changes in the economy and customer demands

- changes in the availability and wage rates of the labour force

- the staff available to work in the accounting function

- the budget applied to the accounting function

If the general or specific economic changes for an organisation lead to an increase or decrease in the general level of transactions then this will have a direct effect on the number of transactions within the accounting function although not necessarily on the nature of those transactions or the method of operations.

Social factors

Social factors that might affect the accounting system might include the following:

- changing work patterns such as flexitime and home working

- family commitments leading to changes such as part time working or job sharing

119

- employment legislation

Technological factors

Examples of technological factors that might cause changes in the accounting system might be:

- advances in computer systems
- security issues
- technological fraud
- on-line banking

HOW IT WORKS

An example of an external economic factor that might affect the accounting system is the fact that two of the major competitors of Angus Bell Ltd have started to offer settlement discounts to selected customers. This could mean that Angus Bell Ltd might also have to offer settlement discounts in order to remain competitive.

If this were the case then this would have a significant effect on the accounting functions. Not only would the preparation of the sales invoices be more complex as the effect of a discount on the VAT charge would have to be taken into account but the sales ledger staff would also have to match payments where discount has been taken to the invoices to ensure that the discount was valid.

SWOT analysis and external factors for change

Earlier in the chapter we considered the use of SWOT analysis to assess an internal control system. The opportunities and threats considered within a SWOT analysis are both largely based upon external factors and could be useful in considering the types of factors that might affect the accounting system.

Activity 7

What does a PEST analysis consist of?

CHAPTER OVERVIEW

- an internal control system is designed to ensure the efficiency of the operations, adherence to management policies, safeguarding of the assets and to ensure the completeness and accuracy of the accounting records

- the individual component elements of the internal control system are the internal controls - there are eight types of internal control - SPAM SOAP - segregation of duties, physical control, authorisation and approval, management controls, supervisory controls, organisational controls, arithmetical and accounting controls, personnel controls

- internal checks are more specific than internal controls and are the checks on the day to day transactions such as pre-lists, post-lists and control totals

- SWOT analysis is a method of assessing an accounting system under the headings of strengths, weaknesses, opportunities and threats

- the accounting function of a business should aim to provide a quality service to both its internal and external customers

- getting it right first time and then getting it more right next time are the basic principles of quality management

- efficiency of the operations of the accounting function can be improved by assessing the current operations and reorganising to make them more efficient

- in order to be cost-effective the work of the accounting department should be carried out at the required level of quality at the lowest possible cost - some of the costs of the accounting function will be controllable by the manager but others will be non-controllable

KEY WORDS

Internal control system   The system of controls, both financial and   otherwise, established by management in order to   carry on the business in an orderly and efficient manner, ensure adherence to management policies,   safeguard the assets and secure as far as   possible the completeness and accuracy of the   records

Internal   controls   The   individual components of an internal control system

Administrative controls   Methods and procedures concerned with the operational efficiency of the business and adherence to management policies

Accounting   controls   Methods   and procedures concerned with safeguarding the assets and ensuring the   completeness, accuracy and reliability of the   financial records

Segregation of duties   An internal control where the aim is that one individual cannot record and process a whole transaction

Internal audit   An independent function of the company reporting to the highest levels of management on the operational efficiency and control system of the business

Internal checks   Checks on day to day transactions

Pre-list   A list of document totals drawn up before the transactions are processed

Post-list   A list of transactions drawn up during or after the processing

Control total   A total of a number of documents or transactions   which is then compared with another total which   should be the same

CHAPTER OVERVIEW

- the manager of an accounting function may wish to make recommendations for improvements in the internal control system, regarding the quality of output, the efficiency of the department or its cost-effectiveness

- the accounting system may require updating either due to internal factors or external factors - one method of identifying relevant external factors is to carry out a PEST analysis

KEY WORDS

SWOT analysis Analysis which considers strengths, weaknesses, opportunities or threats

Quality The degree of excellence of a product or service

Internal customers Functions of the business served by another function of the business

External customers Those outside the organisation for whom products or services are provided

Getting it right first time The key principle of quality management

Efficiency A means of getting the most output for a given level of input

Work study Study of current operations and recommendations for re-organisations that may lead to greater efficiency

Effectiveness The means of achieving the desired objective

Cost-effectiveness Achieving the stated objective at the minimum cost level

Variances The difference between budgeted figures and actual results

Controllable costs Costs over which the manager responsible has some control

Non-controllable costs Costs incurred by a function over which the manager of the function has no control

PEST analysis Analysis of external factors affecting an organisation under the heading of political, economic, social and technological factors

HOW MUCH HAVE YOU LEARNED?

1   Define a system of internal control.

2   What are the eight general types of internal control?

3   What is the aim of segregation of duties within the accounting department?

4   Give two examples of physical controls.

5   What are the two most important features of an internal audit function?

6   Give four examples of arithmetical and accounting controls.

7   What are the main limitations of internal controls?

8   What is SWOT analysis and how can it be applied to the assessment of an accounting system?

9   Who are likely to be the internal customers of an accounts department?

10   What are the four stages in the management of quality?

11   What are the five sets of questions that should be asked about each operation of the accounting function when assessing its efficiency?

12   Give two examples of controllable costs and non-controllable costs which are likely to be incurred in an accounts department.

13   What is a PEST analysis? Give an example of each factor which may affect an accounting system.

chapter 7:
FRAUD WITHIN THE ORGANISATION

chapter coverage

In this chapter we will consider many aspects of fraud, from what it is to how it can be detected. The aim for your project is that you should be able to research into any potential areas of fraud within your accounting system and into fraud risk standards. Towards the end of the chapter we shall consider a matrix approach to grading the various elements of risk of fraud which is the suggested approach in the Guidance Notes to Unit 10.

The topics that we shall cover are:

✍ types of fraud

✍ misappropriation of assets

✍ misstatement of financial statements

✍ common indicators of fraud

✍ assessing risk

✍ detecting fraud

✍ reporting fraud and making recommendations

KNOWLEDGE AND UNDERSTANDING AND PERFORMANCE CRITERIA COVERAGE

knowledge and understanding – the business environment

■ Common types of fraud
■ The implications of fraud

knowledge and understanding – management techniques

■ Methods of fraud detection within accounting systems

Performance criteria – Element 10.1

G Colleagues are encouraged to report promptly to the student any problems and queries that are beyond their authority or expertise to resolve. Students are able to resolve such issues within their own authority and expertise

H Problems and queries beyond a student's own authority or expertise are referred to the appropriate person

Element 10.2

B Potentials areas of fraud, arising from circumventing controls within the accounting system, are identified and their impact graded

D Recommendations are made to the appropriate people in a clear, easily understood format

E Recommendations are supported by a clear rationale which includes an explanation of any assumptions made

TYPES OF FRAUD

Before we start looking in detail at fraud and the various different types that you could come across in a management situation we will start with a consideration of what fraud actually is.

What is fraud?

In simple terms FRAUD is deception of some sort which in a company situation will involve either:

- misappropriation of assets
- misstatement of the financial statements

Misappropriation of assets

In its simplest form misappropriation of assets is the theft of assets such as cash or stock. However there are a variety of different and subtle ways in which this can be accomplished. We will briefly consider each of the following ways of carrying out such fraud:

- theft of cash
- theft of stock
- teeming and lading
- fictitious employees
- fictitious suppliers
- fictitious customers
- collusion with customers
- collusion with suppliers
- receipt of invoices for bogus supply of goods or services
- disposal of assets
- pension funds

Misstatement of the financial statements

In this type of fraud the financial statements are deliberately manipulated in order to falsify the position of the company. This could be by overstating assets or profits or by under-stating the results and the profits.

Examples of this type of fraud will also be considered below:

- over-valuation of stock
- window dressing
- not writing off bad debts
- manipulation of depreciation charges
- fictitious sales
- understating expenses

These lists are not exhaustive but the explanations below will give you an insight into the types of fraud that you should be aware of as possibilities.

MISAPPROPRIATION OF ASSETS

Theft of cash

Most manufacturing or service businesses do not tend to have a large amount of cash around the business premises. However there is always the petty cash, with the associated risk of theft by employees who have access to it.

However in a retail business with cash in a till there is a much greater temptation to steal. A cashier could fairly easily simply not ring up a sale and take the cash from the customer themselves.

Theft of stock

In many organisations employees will pilfer stock. Although ethically wrong these items tend to be of low value and will largely go undetected due to their immaterial nature.

Teeming and lading

TEEMING AND LADING is a common type of fraud within the sales ledger system. It involves stealing of cash or cheques received from customers but is covered up by subsequent receipts being set against the original debt continually rolling over until the perpetrator leaves the organisation with the cash in hand or his fraud is detected.

HOW IT WORKS

A debtor owes £1,000. The sales ledger clerk receives a cheque for £1,000 which he steals and alters to make it payable into his own bank account.

Further sales of £800 are made to this debtor and when the cash is received it is set off against the original £1,000 debt.

Fictitious employees

This fraud works by a fictitious employee being added to the payroll and the weekly or monthly pay being paid into a bank account in this bogus name with the fraudster collecting the money. This will normally only happen in a large organisation where such an additional employee can go by without being noticed.

Other payroll fraud

Individuals within the organisation can falsify their own time sheets in order to be paid more overtime than they actually worked.

Alternatively a member of the payroll department can deliberately inflate the pay of another employee by recording additional hours or using a higher rate of pay.

Fictitious suppliers

In this system a bogus supplier is set up in the records. Invoices are received from this bogus supplier and company cheques made out to pay the supplier but with the money being collected by the fraudster. For this system to work there would need to be very little segregation of duties in the accounting function or collusion between two or more employees.

HOW IT WORKS

In a small accounts department one employee is responsible for placing orders with suppliers, checking the invoices received from the suppliers and authorising payments to those suppliers.

The employee sets up a fictitious supplier, Bloggs & Co, and places an order with this company. An invoice is received from the company for £500, although no goods of course, and the employee authorises payment of this invoice. The cheque is paid into the bank account of Bloggs & Co which was again set up by the employee and the employee has the money.

Fictitious customer

Here a new, but fictitious, customer is set up and allowed credit. Goods are despatched to the customer but collected by the fraudster. The fictitious customer never pays of course and eventually the debt is written off as bad.

For this to work there will normally have to be collusion between the employee taking customer orders and the employee granting credit to new customers or a situation where one employee is responsible for both roles.

Collusion with customers

This is a system where both the customer and the employee benefit at the business's expense by splitting between them any gains made by the customer. This may be done by an employee in the accounts department charging lower prices on the invoice to the customer than the true value of the goods or by a member of the stores staff under-recording the amount delivered to the customer.

HOW IT WORKS

1,000 units of a product are delivered to a customer, French Ltd. However the invoice clerk invoices the customer for only 500 units of the product as there is no independent check from sales order to sales invoices. The goods are invoiced at £20 each and the £10,000 gain made by French Ltd is split between that company and the invoice clerk.

Collusion with suppliers

Here a supplier invoices the business for more goods than were actually received or for a higher value. The supplier is paid the inflated amount and the gain is split between the supplier and the fraudulent employee.

HOW IT WORKS

Goods with a value of £2,000 are received from a supplier. However the supplier's invoice is for £3,000. The payments clerk is in collusion with the supplier and authorises the payment of £3,000 and receives his share of the £1,000 gain made by the supplier.

Receipt of invoices for bogus supply of goods or services

The business receives an invoice for supply of goods, or more commonly services such as consultancy fees. The goods or services were never of course received. The invoice is paid but it is to the account of a fraudulent employee who sent the invoice.

Disposal of assets

In some cases an employee may buy an asset from the business such as computer or a car for personal use. If the net book value of the asset manipulated to be lower than the market value, by over-depreciation for example, then the employee will be charged a lower price than the worth of the asset thereby defrauding the business.

Pension funds

Pension funds can be open to misuse for example by the company using pension fund assets or transferring company assets to the pension fund at an over-valued amount.

Activity 1

What is meant by teeming and lading?

MISSTATEMENT OF THE FINANCIAL STATEMENTS

Over valuation of stock

This is a method of inflating net assets and profits by over-valuing the closing stock of the business. As this tends to be a subjective area this can be done in a variety of ways:

- pre-year end deliveries to customers or returns to suppliers may be not be recorded

- stock lines may be deliberately miscounted

- obsolete stock may remain in the books at cost rather than being written down to net book value

- individual stock lines may simply be valued at a higher value than their actual cost.

Window dressing

WINDOW DRESSING is the manipulation of events at the year end in order to improve the appearance of the financial statements. Methods include the following:

- over invoicing before the year end and issuing credit notes after the year end

- not recording purchases of goods just before the year end until after the year end

- deliberately not paying suppliers before the year end in order to increase the cash balance or decrease the overdraft

Not writing off bad debts

Any long-standing bad debts should be written off. If this does not happen the asset base of the company is over-stated and the profit is greater.

Manipulation of depreciation charges

If depreciation rates which are lower than they should be are applied to the fixed assets then this will lead to a higher net book value and higher profits than if the true depreciation rate were used.

Fictitious sales

Invoicing bogus customers before the year end and then sending out credit notes after the year end or writing off the debt after the year end will increase profits and debtors for the current year.

Understating expenses

If expenses are omitted from the financial records or accruals not accounted for at the year end this will overstate both profits and net assets.

Financial statements

These last six types of fraud are intended to misstate the financial statements. In the examples given above it has been assumed that the intention was to overstate profits and assets. However by carrying out each fraud in reverse it would of course be possible to understate profits and net assets if that was required, for example for tax or business valuation purposes.

Activity 2

What is meant by window dressing?

COMMON INDICATORS OF FRAUD

In the next few sections we will be considering the assessment of the risk of fraud within the accounting system and the detection of fraud. No system can ever be fraudproof and it will be impossible to eliminate fraud completely. However as a manager, your starting point is to be aware of a number of common indicators which may alert you to the fact that something is not quite right:

- corporate culture
- size and organisation structure
- changes in profit levels
- individual employee's behaviour
- excessive hours
- expensive lifestyle
- management style
- staff problems
- targets and budgets
- administration issues
- accounting problems

Corporate culture

The attitude within an organisation, or its CORPORATE CULTURE, can make a contribution to whether it is a high or low risk environment for fraud. A culture where small unethical practices such as stealing of stationery or false expense claims are tolerated may in turn lead to larger frauds by employees or higher levels of management. If a company has a clear anti-fraud policy then this may lead to a culture within the organisation which does not tolerate fraud of any size or at any level.

Size and organisation structure

A large organisation is sometimes more likely to suffer fraudulent activities as it is easier for employees to be anonymous and for transactions to get lost. Equally if there is a complex organisation structure this may increase the likelihood of fraud.

However in a small organisation there will tend to be a lack of segregation of duties and this again can facilitate fraud.

A lack of management supervision or a lack of clear management control of responsibility, authority and delegation may also be indicative of potential for fraudulent activities.

Changes in profit levels

If profit levels show a decrease and appear to be suddenly significantly lower than competitors this may be an indication of the misappropriation of assets or possibly of deliberate misstatement of the financial statements.

If profit levels suddenly increase, or sales rise without a proportionate increase in costs this may be evidence of the creation of fictitious customers collusion with customers or manipulation of the financial statements.

Activity 3

How can corporate culture affect the likelihood of fraud taking place in an organisation?

Individual employees' behaviour

Few people are brazen enough to carry out fraud without there being some hint of this in their behaviour. Some employees may become excessively secretive about their duties at work whereas others involved in fraud may become irritable if anyone questions them, however innocently, about their tasks or role. As a manager you should be alert to unusual, irrational or inconsistent behaviour.

Excessive hours

If an employee is perpetrating a fraud they run the risk of it being discovered if anyone else carries out their tasks even for a short period of time. Therefore employees who work excessively long hours, refuse to take holidays or insist that certain tasks should not be carried out until they return from holiday may potentially be involved in fraudulent activities.

Expensive lifestyle

This is one of the most common indicators of fraud. An employee suddenly appears to be living a lifestyle which would normally be beyond their means - cars, holidays, moving house etc. Such things may be flaunted at work and excuses such as a sudden inheritance given but, as a manager, it may put you on your guard.

Management style

Detecting fraud can be extremely difficult when it is being perpetrated by a senior member of the management team or a director. If such a person has an autocratic management style, wide ranging powers, a dominant personality and is very senior in the organisation it is the rare, lower level manager or employee who will question his actions, so their fraudulent activities can carry on for a considerable period of time without being detected.

Staff problems

Another common cause of individual employees carrying out fraudulent activities is a grudge against their employer. If employees feel that they are not sufficiently remunerated or they have been passed over for promotion this can be a strong motive for an individual with the opportunity to commit a fraud.

An environment where there are dissatisfied staff, low salary levels for key staff, personal financial pressures on key staff or potential labour force reductions or redundancies, may be much more susceptible to fraud.

Targets and budgets

In many organisations the overall remuneration of managers and key employees may be dependent upon their meeting high or aggressive targets or budget figures. Where management compensation is highly dependent upon meeting such targets there may be temptation to manipulate the financial accounting figures in order to appear to meet such targets.

Administration issues

Some fairly simple administrative issues may be indicators of a possible fraud. If documents and records are being frequently altered or there is extensive use of correction fluid or the production of photocopies of documents rather than originals these may be indicators that something is wrong. Other potential indicators might be stamps rather than original signatures, signature or handwriting discrepancies or transactions which are taking place without the appropriate authorisation.

Accounting problems

As we saw in the previous chapter there will be many internal checks built into the internal control system designed to find errors or potential frauds. If these checks highlight problems then this may be an indicator of fraud. For example, control accounts which cannot be reconciled, unreconciling bank reconciliations, unexplained stock adjustments or confirmation letters not returned from suppliers or customers.

Project note

Although as a manager you should be alert to the types of indicators listed above, take care in your project not to jump to conclusions in every circumstance. It does not mean that every time an employee seems to be working excessive overtime without taking leave that he is committing a fraud, although it is possible.

Activity 4

What type of staff problems might make a company more susceptible to fraudulent activity?

ASSESSING RISK

As well as being aware of the types of fraud that exist and the most common indicators of fraud, as detailed above, managers should be aware that one of the key deterrents to fraudulent activities is a strong internal control system. However in most systems there will be weaknesses and a manager may be required to carry out a RISK ASSESSMENT for all or part of the accounting system to try to determine the nature and level of any risk of fraud.

There are several stages in this risk assessment with regard to fraud:

- establish a risk management group
- identify risk areas
- analyse fraud risks
- assess the scale of risk
- develop and implement a risk management strategy

Establish a risk management group

A RISK MANAGEMENT GROUP (RMG) should be established to conduct a review of the risks of fraud that the organisation faces and to be responsible for reviewing systems and procedures, identifying and assessing risks and introducing controls best suited to the situation.

The group will need to assess the organisation's RISK APPETITE which is the level of risk that the organisation is prepared to accept.

The members of the RMG should be individuals with expertise in the company's systems and procedures, a basic knowledge of fraud and the knowledge and authority to introduce changes to procedures and new controls. This is likely to include the finance director, other senior accounting personnel and normally at least one non-finance individual to bring a different perspective to the group.

Identifying risk areas

For Unit 10 you are concerned about the accounting system and therefore the risk areas that you will normally need to consider will include the following:

- the sales cycle
- the purchases cycle
- the payroll cycle
- cash payments
- cash receipts
- expenses
- stock
- fixed assets

For each of these areas of the accounting system you will need to consider the internal control system for this area and the types of internal control that exist in that area. If there is a lack of internal controls or the internal controls do not appear to be being implemented then this could be an area that is at risk of fraud.

Activity 5

Who are likely to be the appointed members of a risk management group?

Analyse fraud risks

For each of the areas of the accounting system considered there should be assessment of the risks of either false accounting or misappropriation of cash or other assets. This is often done using a matrix approach as developed by Ernst and Young, known as the ERNST AND YOUNG MODEL.

Department or area	Details of risk area	Management	Employees	Third parties	Collusion

Using this model for each section of the accounting system the risk of fraud by management, employees or third parties can be considered as well as the risk of collusion of parties to perpetrate a fraud.

HOW IT WORKS

In a purchase ledger system in a small accounts department the purchase ledger clerk is responsible for the issuing of purchase orders and checking o purchase orders to suppliers' invoices. The accountant is responsible fo authorising payment to suppliers and for signing the cheques. The accountan is also responsible for checking the financial viability of any new suppliers The risk of fraud in this system might be analysed as follows:

Department or area	Details of risk area	Management	Employees	Third parties	Collusion
Purchase ledger	False suppliers set up and paid		Accountant		PL clerk
Purchase ledger	Inflated charges from supplier		Accountant	Supplier	PL clerk

Assess the scale of risk

Once risk areas have been identified then an assessment must be made o both the possible impact of the particular risk and the likelihood of it occurrence.

The risk assessment should not just consider the financial risk but also the organisation's viability and reputation and any political or commercia sensitivities involved.

When grading the likelihood of the risk it is common practice to analyse it a follows:

- high - probable
- medium - possible
- low - remote

The assessment of the risk could be considered in matrix form like this

Area of risk	Probability	Impact	Controls	Net likely impact	Action

HOW IT WORKS

Using the previous purchase ledger system the risks could be assessed as follows:

Area of risk	Probability	Impact	Controls	Net likely impact	Action
False suppliers set up and paid	Medium	High	Low	Medium	Further controls required
Inflated charges from supplier	High	High	Low	High	Priority investigstion

Develop and implement a risk management strategy

Once the organisation's risk appetite has been set and the risk areas identified and assessed, the RMG can begin to develop strategies to deal with each risk area. The aim will be to introduce cost-effective controls to minimise the risks. There is a cost to combating risk so the use of the matrix approach above will help to determine the most appropriate strategies.

Within the accounting system this will probably be to ignore small risks although to keep them under review and to deal with risk reduction by the introduction of further controls and procedures.

The strategy chosen must then be communicated to those responsible for their implementation and responsibility assigned to the appropriate manager. Target dates should be set for each action to be implemented and the success of these controls in meeting their objectives must be monitored.

Activity 6

What is meant by a company's risk appetite?

DETECTING FRAUD

The main responsibility for the prevention and detection of fraud is that of the management of the entity, the directors and managers. They should establish and maintain policies and procedures which are there to ensure, as far as possible, the orderly and efficient conduct of the business. This responsibility includes the implementation and operation of the accounting and internal control systems which are designed to prevent and detect fraud and error.

It is also important to raise awareness of fraud though education and training of managers and in particular those operating in high risk areas such as stock purchases and payments.

Detection of fraud in practice

Ernst and Young carried out a survey into the methods of detecting fraudulent activities in practice and the results are illustrated in the graph below:

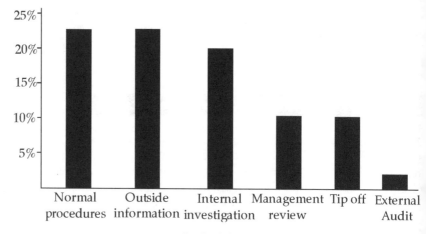

Method of detection

It is clear from this that most frauds are discovered through the operation of the normal systems of control or as a result of information received from outsiders who are often ex-employees. Detection of fraud is everyone's responsibility and consideration of some of the common indicators of fraud considered earlier in the chapter may help in this.

Project note

As a manager you should be aware of the possibility of fraud through your knowledge of the systems and procedures in place within your area of expertise. You should always also have the mindset that 'fraud is always an option' when considering a problem area.

REPORTING FRAUD AND MAKING RECOMMENDATIONS

If fraud is suspected by any individual within an organisation it is important that there is a defined and well known procedure for dealing with this.

Fraud response plan

FRAUD RESPONSE PLAN is a formal means of setting down the procedures for dealing with any suspected case of theft, misappropriation or falsifying of accounting records. Such a plan can also help with its deterrent value and give employees more confidence to come forward if any form of fraud is suspected.

The fraud response plan is the means by which the organisation's attitude to fraud is communicated to all employees, managers, directors and even shareholders.

Fraud officer

In many large organisations a senior manager is employed as the company FRAUD OFFICER. His duties would include the following:

- receive information from staff confidentially and if necessary anonymously

- provide advice to individuals who have suspicions

- implementing the fraud response plan

- be responsible for initiating and overseeing any fraud investigations

- liaising with any necessary third parties

- any further follow up actions

It is an important requisite of the job that the fraud officer does not require approval from senior management for his actions.

In many smaller organisations however the most senior person to report any suspected fraud to is the finance director.

Project note

As a manager you should be aware of how to deal with any case of suspected fraud which comes to your attention. You should have a list of contacts which may include senior management or a fraud officer.

Activity 7

What is a fraud response plan?

Whistleblowing

In many cases fraud in an organisation is known about or suspected by number of people who are not involved. However these people will ofte not want to become involved for a variety of fairly simple emotional reasons

- suspicion not proof
- fear of consequences
- working group loyalties
- family loyalties

It is a difficult aspect of any job, but it is important that junior members staff are encouraged to report any suspected areas of fraudulent activity this may be an indication of fraud at any level which can be taken up by the management of the organisation.

One of the aims of an organisation should be that its anti-fraud culture an reporting processes actually do encourage whistleblowers. However there often a fear of the consequences of whistleblowing which may stop individu employees from reporting any suspicions. Managers should try to instil belief that it is everyone's responsibility to combat fraud for the good of th organisation and indeed potentially to save their own jobs.

Project note

As a manager you should actively consider whether your staff would happily come to you about a problem at work that had raised their suspicions in any way.

The manager's role

From your viewpoint as a manager if any unusual or suspicious activity reported to you then you must always take it seriously and consid investigation. Even anonymous accusations should be considered befo being dismissed in case they are valid, but the organisation's manageme might consider stating in the fraud policy that such anonymous accusation will be treated with caution.

Upon carrying out a basic investigation into the suspected activities it is the important that managers should refer the matter to a higher level of authorit A manager to whom suspicious activity is reported should only act within th limits of his own authority and expertise and should then report the matte together with any information or evidence that he has to a highe management level.

CHAPTER OVERVIEW

- fraud within a company can either result in a misappropriation of assets or a deliberate misstatement of the financial statements

- a manager should always be aware that fraud might be taking place and should look for a number of common indicators of something not being quite right

- a manager may also be required to carry out a risk assessment for fraud which will involve establishing a risk management group, identifying risk areas, analysing fraud risks, assessing the scale of risk and developing and implementing a fraud risk management strategy

- fraud is generally detected through the normal procedures and systems of the organisation so the internal control system is of key importance

- a fraud response plan is a strategy for encouraging all employees to report any suspicions that they may have of fraudulent activity

KEY WORDS

Fraud Deception which results in the misappropriation of assets or the misstatement of the financial statements

Teeming and lading Fraud within the sales ledger system where money from debtors is misappropriated and then covered by subsequent receipts set against the original debt

Window dressing Deliberate manipulation of the financial statements at the year end

Corporate culture The general attitude and philosophies within an organisation

Risk assessment An assessment to determine the nature and level of risk of fraud within the accounting system or part of it

Risk management group A senior and experienced group of manager from both the accounting and non-accounting functions responsible for identifying, assessing and managing the risk of fraud

Risk appetite The level of risk that the organisation is prepared to accept

Ernst and Young Model A matrix approach model to assessing and analysing the risk of fraud developed by Ernst and Young

Fraud response plan A formal means of setting down the procedures for dealing with any suspected cases of fraud

Fraud officer Senior manager within the organisation responsible for all aspects of fraud management

HOW MUCH HAVE YOU LEARNED?

1   What are the two types of fraud that a company might encounter?

2   Briefly explain three methods of how assets might be misappropriated from a company.

3   Briefly explain three methods of how the financial statements might be deliberate misstated.

4   Briefly explain three common indicators of fraud.

5   What are the stages in a fraud risk assessment?

6   What are the main risk areas in the accounting system?

7   What is a risk management group and what are its responsibilities?

8   What is the role of a fraud officer?

chapter 8:
WRITING YOUR REPORT

FINDING A REPORT TOPIC

The aims of Unit 10

Before we consider your report in any detail we will put it into perspectiv
by considering the overall aims of the Unit 10 Standards of Competence.

Element 10.1 is about managing people within an accounting environmer
and Element 10.2 is concerned with identifying opportunities for improvin
the effectiveness of an accounting system, including identifying and assessir
potential areas of fraud. Therefore when planning the subject matter of you
report bear in mind that it should be based within an accountir
environment but is concerned not only with the accounting system but als
with the management of the people within that accounting environment.

Unit 10 emphasises the student's understanding of the role of managers in th
accounting environment, whether this is as a line manager or as a manage
of a specific project or function.

Nature of the report

The project for Unit 10 is to write a report to management which analyse
the management accounting system and the skills of the people workir
within it. The report should identify how both the system and the skills of th
people can be enhanced to improve their effectiveness. In producing th
report you will need to prove competence in:

- the coordination of work activities
- the identification and grading of fraud in the system
- identification of weaknesses in the system
- recommendations for improvements to the system
- monitoring and reviewing changes for their effectiveness

The total length of the report should not exceed 4,000 words and th
includes any appendices that there may be. The report should be approve
by an appropriate manager and that manager should attest to its originalit
authenticity and its quality.

Management experience

Not all students who are studying Unit 10 will have actual experience as
line manager or project or function manager, so the Guidance Notes to th
unit give three possible bases upon which you can be assessed for the unit

- if a student has experience as a manager in an accountir
  environment the report can be written on the basis of that first han
  experience.

- If a student has no actual experience of management but has observed managers in action in an accounting environment they can use those observations and analyses of the managers' actions as the basis for their report

- if a student cannot write a report on either of the first two bases then the report can be based upon an AAT simulation in the form of a case study. (A copy of the AAT sample simulation is given later in this text in the Revision Companion element together with a suggested report based upon that simulation).

the report is to be written on either of the first two bases then it should be ased upon an actual management accounting system, or part-system within our workplace in the present or recent past. For students who are not in elevant employment the guidance notes state that an unpaid placement uch as a voluntary organisation or charity, club or society or a college epartment may be suitable.

herefore the first stage in the planning of your report topic is to determine hether you have actual or observed management experiences on which to ase your report or whether your report must be based upon an AAT mulation case study.

Choosing a topic for your report

uidance notes for Unit 10 state clearly that all the Performance Criteria and nowledge and Understanding for the unit must be addressed either in your port content or by additional documented assessor questioning. Therefore our report should aim to cover as many of the Performance Criteria as ossible as this will usually also mean that the Knowledge and Understanding ave also been addressed.

herefore as a starting point to planning the topic and content of your report e will summarise the important factors, as many of which as possible should e covered in the report. Ideally your report should provide evidence that ou have planned and undertaken each of the following:

- work routines to meet organisational time schedules and to make the best use of both human and physical resources. The actual planning and scheduling of your report for completion to an appropriate standard and on time will provide some evidence of this

- the systematic review of staff competencies and training needs together with details of any training actually arranged.

- contingency planning, in collaboration with management, for possible emergencies

- the clear communication of work methods and schedules to colleagues so that they have an understanding of what is expected of them

- the monitoring of work activities sufficiently closely against standard to ensure they are being met

- the coordination of work activities effectively against workplans an contingency plans

- the encouragement of colleagues to report promptly any issue beyond their authority and expertise, resolving these where possibl or otherwise referring such issues to the appropriate person

- a situation analysis of the accounting system under scrutiny

- evidence of resulting recommendations made to the appropria people in a clear, understandable format and supported by a clea rationale with all assumptions clearly stated

- research into any potential areas of fraud within the accountir system and into appropriate fraud risk standards. Here it recommended that you use some form of matrix approach toward grading the various elements of risk (see Chapter 7)

- a regular review of methods of operating

- updates to the system which, where appropriate, have been mac in accordance with both internal factors and external factors th require such updates to be made.

This may seem like an awful lot to be covered by one 4,000 word report s we will now summarise the requirements into key topics which you can loc back to in the Course Companion if you so wish.

Summary of the key contents of the report

- planning and scheduling
- review of staff competencies
- contingency planning
- communication
- monitoring and coordination of work activities
- a SWOT analysis of the accounting system
- recommendations for improvements in the system
- research into potential areas of fraud
- updates to the system using SWOT analysis for internal factors ar PEST analysis for relevant external factors

At this stage you should now spend some time considering your wo experiences and determining which of these can be used in order to form th basis for a report which covers as many of the key topics stated above possible.

PLANNING THE REPORT

Once you have decided upon the topic and the context in which your report is to be written the planning stage begins. The secret of producaing a good report is adequate planning and a good structure. The planning stage of your report could well take up to a third of the total time that you will spend on it but it is time well spent.

Structure of the report

In order to plan your report you will need to have an idea of what the report is going to look like when you have finished. A typical formal report will have the following sections:

Title

This seems fairly obvious but it is important that the title succinctly summarises what your report is about so that as soon as someone starts to read it they have it in context - do not use the title of Unit 10 instead make it specific to the areas that you are reporting on.

Contents

You will need a contents sheet which may be cross referenced by page number or paragraph number so that a reader can easily refer to it and find specific elements of the report - this cannot be written until the report has been completed.

Summary

It may seem strange to have a summary at the beginning of the report but this is very useful for busy managers who see the title of the report, the contents and then the summary and can then prioritise how urgent it is for them to read the entire report. Again this part of the report cannot be written until the main body of the report has been completed.

Terms of reference

This section effectively puts the report into context. It will explain why the report has been written, its scope, what it covers and what it does not cover.

When you have completed your report, refer back to these terms of reference to ensure that all objectives have been covered.

Methodology

Whilst preparing your report you will no doubt be collecting and analysing data. In this section of the report you must explain the steps you have taken to do this, the documents or computer records consulted, the people you have spoken to and the computations or analyses that you have carried out.

Body of the report

Now you are on to the main body of the report which should start with an introduction to the company, the department or the section which the report is based upon.

Once the report has been set into context in the introduction the remainder of the report should set out your findings and the information discovered. As you will need to cover a number of Performance Criteria in your report it is likely that it will cover a number of different topics each of which should be clearly headed up and dealt with in a logical order.

Conclusions

In this section of the report all of the information gathered in the report brought together and you will have to come to a conclusion on those findings.

Recommendations

As a direct result of the conclusions from your report it is anticipated that you will make recommendations as to the improvement of the system or to the skills or working patterns of the people working in the accounting environment. The recommendations will be an essential part of your report and should be presented in a logical order. Any recommendations should clearly state how the current system works, the recommendation for change, the reasons for such a change, the costs and benefits of such change and any assumptions made when deciding upon the recommendations.

Appendices

The main body of the report does not need to be filled with detailed calculations, tables of figures or findings or copies of relevant original documents. These will be referred to in the main body of the report but should be reported at the back of the report as appendices and cross referenced in the main body of the report.

Producing a plan for your report

Once you know the structure of your report then you can start thinking about its content. Using the Performance Criteria and the key areas that we discussed earlier in the chapter you should be able to note down the areas that you wish to cover in your report. For example a SWOT analysis of the sales system, potential areas of fraud in the sales system, an analysis of the competencies of your staff, a PERT analysis to identify changes in the system etc.

Once you have noted down all of these ideas then you should consider the order in which to report them to ensure that your report follows a logical order. At this stage you should have the main headings for your report. You might wish to use a check list of the Performance Criteria to check that you have covered as many as possible.

Now you need to consider how you will find the information that you wish to include in your report. You may need to carry out investigations, collect data, find documents, arrange meetings, make telephone calls, assess computer files or manual documents, carry out analyses and computations etc. Each of these tasks should be planned for in terms of hours required, documents required, computer time required.

Remember that the planning and scheduling that you carry out in preparation of your report will provide evidence towards meeting the Performance Criteria regarding work routines and meeting organisational time schedules.

PRESENTATION OF YOUR REPORT

Knowing what is going into your report and what it is going to look like is only part of the process. The report must be written well too. A report is a form of communication and therefore as with any form of communication you should aim to get your message across clearly and accurately.

Language and style

The type of language that you use in your report and style of your writing will be of almost as much importance as the actual content of the report. Given below are some pointers on how to communicate in writing in a clear and effective manner.

Length of the report

Although 4,000 words may seem a lot it is very easy to overrun this limit. Try to make your report as brief as it possibly can be without losing any information. This can be achieved by using short words rather than longer ones wherever possible and short, succinct sentences.

Clear wording

Try to avoid using complex words or phrases - they are much harder to read and understand than simple words and statements.

Jargon and slang

Wherever possible avoid using jargon which may not be readily understood by the person using the report. In general simple accounting terms can be assumed to be understood by management such as segregation of duties or batch processing.

Slang words and 'in-phrases' should be avoided.

'Janet Jones is happy in her work'

is preferable to:

'Janet Jones is cool'

Objectivity

Try to avoid writing in the first person - avoid using 'I' or 'you'

'The productivity decline in the department should be looked into further'

is preferable to:

'In my view I think that you should investigate the productivity decline in th. department'

Take care when writing your report to ensure that it does not conta personal feelings and opinions. If you are writing the report based upc either personal experience as a manager or on the basis of observations another manager then it is very easy to fall into the trap of allowing person bias to creep into your report. You are writing this report from yo company's point of view and focusing on your company's needs therefore c not use it as a forum for verbalising personal views on systems, staff management.

Diagrams

You may find it useful to use diagrams such as flowcharts in your report. F example if you are describing an element of the accounting system document flowchart can be useful. However take care only to use su diagrams where appropriate and in most cases put them in an appenc rather than in the main body of the report.

Drafting the report

Once you have gathered the information and analyses that you need for yo report then you should have a go at the first draft of the report. You may w alter this considerably at a later stage but try to get on with the first draft soon as you can. This will not only make you feel as though you are maki progress but also allow a rough word count so that you know whether y need to expand on the report or to cut it down.

You will then work on the initial draft report until you are happy that the fir report is of the right quality, style and length.

General presentation

First impressions are important - make sure that the report that you submit is not crumpled or dirty or covered in yesterday's lunch.

Use the spell check facility of your computer or word processor to ensure that there are no spelling mistakes. Having done that, read through your report again yourself (or ask someone else to do so) as the spell check will only pick up wrongly spelt words, not correctly spelt words wrongly used.

Break up any longer sections of the report by using headings. Make sure any heading is informative and does tell the reader what the next section of the report is about.

Your report is likely to cover a number of separate areas and topics therefore use headings and subparagraph headings as much as possible for the sake of clarity and ease of reading.

Appendices

The main body of your report should be limited to the details of your investigations and findings. Any additional material such as calculations, spreadsheets, analyses, diagrams, flowcharts, documents such as job descriptions, should be relegated to appendices at the end of the report and the main body of the report should be cross-referenced to these appendices.

Accuracy and precision

A final word on accuracy - remember to check and double check all figures and calculations. An error in the calculation of any key figures could affect any conclusions that you draw or any recommendations that you make.

Also make sure that you are precise in the wording that you use and avoid vague generalisations. For example 'some of the invoices tested for authorisation do not appear to have been properly authorised' is too vague. What would be preferable would be 'of the 20 invoices tested for authorisation 2 were not properly authorised'.

Also take care when making any recommendations that these are clear and precise. 'Ken Barton could do with some more computer training' is far too imprecise however 'it is recommended that Ken Barton attends the next available in house computer spreadsheet course' is much better.

GUIDANCE FOR UNIT 10

The AAT issue Guidance Notes for Unit 10 and as part of these they set ou the role of the Approved Assessment Centre and that of the student ir producing this report. Both of these are reproduced below and may be helpful to you whilst carrying out the project report for this unit.

The Approved Assessment Centre's role (AAC)

The AAC should undertake the following steps:

- make an initial assessment of the project idea

- use one-to-one sessions to advise and support the student

- encourage workplace mentors to participate (testimony etc)

- ensure the project is the student's original work

- use formative assessments and action plans to guide the student

- undertake summative assessment against performance criteria range statements and knowledge and understanding

- sign off each performance criteria

- conduct a final assessment interview with documented questionin;

The student's role

The student should ensure that the project's format is such that it:

- covers all performance criteria, range statements and knowledg and understanding (perhaps use a tick list to tick off eac performance criteria and knowledge and understanding as it covered in your report)

- covers the objectives set out in the terms of reference of the proje

- is well laid out, easy to read and includes an executive summary

- uses report form style with appropriate language

- shows clear progression from one idea to the next

- cross-refers the main text to any appendices

- uses diagrams and flowcharts appropriately

- starts each section on a fresh page.

The student should ensure that the project's content is such that:

- issues and objectives are clearly identified

- the current situation is clearly analysed

- recommendations are subjected to cost-benefit analysis

- key data is included, and superfluous detail omitted

- the methodology is fully described

- a strategic approach is taken

- the project focuses on company needs, not personal feelings.

Each of these ideas have been covered in this chapter but this serves as a convenient checklist for you when you get to the end of your report to ensure that you have covered all aspects that are required for Unit 10.

ANSWERS

Chapter 1 Organisational structure

1   Personal answer required

2   Personal answer required

3   ■   shareholders/investors
     ■   providers of loan finance
     ■   customers
     ■   suppliers
     ■   the government
     ■   the community

4   As the European Community moves towards greater harmonisation of accounting standards there is agreement that from 2005 many UK and other European companies must prepare their financial statements according to International Accounting Standards.

5   **Mission statement - accounting function**

     The objective of the accounting function is to process all transactions of the business accurately, completely and securely. This will then allow the function to prepare financial accounting information and management accounting information as and when it is required in the format that is most useful and relevant.

Chapter 2 Planning and co-ordinating work

1   An objective is an aim of the business whereas a strategy is a method of achieving that objective.

2   A routine task is one that is part of the daily, weekly or monthly routine of an individual's job. Routine tasks might include listing the cheques each morning as they arrive in the post, or the monthly preparation of the purchase ledger control account reconciliation.

     An unexpected task is a task that is not a routine task but one that must be completed. An example might be preparation of salesmens' expenses for the last month for the sales director or a one off report for the managing director.

3   An urgent task is one for which there is a deadline which is very close. For example it is 3.00pm and all sales invoices for the day must be printed and posted by 4.30pm or figures must be prepared for the financial controller for a meeting with the finance director first thing tomorrow.

     An important task is one which must be carried out and for which an employee is responsible but which is not yet urgent. For example if today is Monday then the petty cash book summary due for Friday is important but not urgent. Again if today is Monday and the financial controller requested information about customer account balances for Wednesday afternoon and thes balances will take only an hour or so to prepare, this is important but not urgent.

4   Factors to be taken into account when allocating tasks to team members:

- use any specialist to do the specialist work in preference to other work

- if only one individual can perform a task use them for that task in preference to othe tasks

- be sensitive to individuals skills and likes and dislikes when allocating tasks

- ensure that boring or mundane tasks are not always allocated to the same person.

5   Deadlines, on the whole, will have been set for a reason. Normally this is done because th results of the task in question are needed by someone else in the organisation by a specific tim in order for them to carry out their tasks. Therefore deadlines should be met in order to ensu that everyone in the organisation is able to carry out their tasks to the correct timescale.

6   The main roles of the project manager are:

- to plan the project in overview and to ensure that it can be completed on time

- to schedule the tasks involved in the project to ensure that the project is completed c time

- to allocate the tasks to individual team members

- to coordinate the work of the individual team members and to ensure that all tasks a being completed within the timescale

- to monitor the progress of team members and the project and to take corrective acti where necessary.

7   The main principles of effective time management are:

- set goals to break down your overall job into its specific tasks

- make plans to determine how to achieve those goals

- make lists detailing what must be achieved each week and each day

- set priorities and deal with the most urgent and important tasks first

- concentrate on one task at a time and wherever possible complete that task befc moving on

- do not put off large, tedious or difficult jobs - get them done now.

Chapter 3 Managing a team

1   A departmental manager as a permanent manager of the same team will be fully aware of t teams members' capabilities and practices. However a project manager may not know t individual members of his project team and indeed the team may be made up of special rather than accountants.

2   Sells style of leadership

3   The four main principles of supervision are:

- authority - you can only supervise if you have the authority to do so - official authority comes from your position within the company eg accounts supervisor, but unofficially your authority comes from your leadership style and the way in which you conduct yourself. To be in authority over others means that you must have their respect. Authority gives you the right to instruct your team members to act as you wish

- responsibility - with authority comes responsibility. This means that you are responsible for the actions of those whom you authorise to carry out tasks

- discipline - as a supervisor not only must you ensure that those working for you behave within the standards required but also that you set an example of good behaviour and work practices

- merit - individuals within the team must be praised or rewarded on the basis of their performance. Under-achievers should not be rewarded or praised, but possibly helped, whilst those achieving targets should be recognised.

4   In many instances managers and supervisors find it difficult to delegate tasks and this can be for any of the following reasons:

- lack of faith in the ability of assistants to carry out the tasks to the manager or supervisor's standards

- concern about the effects of mistakes by assistants and the costs of putting those mistakes right

- the manager or supervisor may feel a need to stay in touch with the workings of the team by carrying out tasks that could be delegated.

5   In these circumstances the most appropriate method of communication would be a face to face interview in private. The factors that should be considered before this interview would include:

- ensure that your facts are correct

- ensure that the assistant realises that this is an interview to assess his performance

- take care not to use any inappropriate body language

- be prepared to listen to any explanations that the assistant has

- make sure that the assistant fully understands the problem and clarify any further action that is to be taken.

6   A team is a group that is formed for a particular purpose and unlike other groups of employees it has a specific purpose, a task or tasks to perform and a sense of identity.

7   Hygiene factors may include pay, bonuses, working conditions, job security, company policy, culture and administration and quality of supervision.

Motivator factors include responsibility, challenges, achievement, status, promotion, recognition and personal growth.

Chapter 4 Competence and training

1   The main stages of a typical appraisal scheme are:

- setting the criteria for assessment
- preparing the appraisal report
- the appraisal interview
- the assessment review
- preparation of an action plan
- the follow up process.

2   Specific

   Measurable

   Agreed

   Realistic

   Time-bounded

   Evaluated

   Reviewed

3   (i)   External course

   (ii)   Internal course if resources are available or external course if not

   (iii) Computer based training - eg Mavis Beacon

   (iv)   On the job training

Chapter 5 Contingency plans

1   Contingency planning is the assessment of the probability of a risk or event occurring and of the effect this will have on the business. If the probability is reasonable and the effect material then a plan must be considered to limit the effect if the event were to take place.

2   For password control to be effective in a computer system the following controls must exercised:

- passwords should be confidential
- passwords should be kept hidden and private
- passwords should be changed regularly
- passwords should not be obvious.

3   Multi skilled employees are employees who are trained not just to perform their own special tasks but also the tasks of other employees within the department or section. Multi skill employees can be extremely useful in cases of staff absence whereby the tasks of the absent employee can be carried out by other members of staff.

Chapter 6 Improvements to the accounting system

1   The four main aims of an internal control system are to:

- ensure the efficiency of the operations
- ensure adherence to management policies
- safeguard the assets
- ensure completeness and accuracy of the accounting records.

2   The eight general controls are:

- Segregation of duties
- Physical controls
- Authorisation and approval
- Management controls
- Supervisory controls
- Organisational controls
- Arithmetical and accounting controls
- Personnel controls

3   Strengths   - monthly control account reconciliations
    Weaknesses   - lack of segregation of duties
    Opportunities   - introduction of a new computer system
    Threats   - potential for fraudulent activities

4
- sending out sales invoices/credit notes promptly
- prompt paying in of monies received
- sending out of reports to management which are accurate and timely

5   Efficiency is the means of getting the most output for a given level of input.

6   Cost-effectiveness is a means of achieving the stated objectives at the lowest possible cost.

7   Analysis under the following headings:

- Political factors
- Economic factors
- Social factors
- Technological factors

Chapter 7 Fraud within the organisation

1   Teeming and lading is a fraud within the sales ledger system whereby cash or cheques received from customers are stolen by a sales ledger employee but the theft is covered up by the subsequent receipts being set against the original debt and this system being rolled over for each subsequent receipt.

2   Window dressing is the manipulation of year end accounting events in order to improve the appearance of the financial statements.

3   Corporate culture is the attitude that pervades an organisation. Where the corporate culture turns a blind eye to minor unethical practices such as stealing stationery it is more likely that larger frauds will take place. However in a company with a clear anti-fraud policy at any level and to any degree there is less likelihood of fraud taking place.

4   Staff problems might be specific such as an individual employee with a grudge against the company, for example an employee who has been passed over for promotion, who might be tempted to get back at the employer by perpetrating a fraud. Staff problems may also be more widespread, such as low salary levels generally or imminent staff redundancies, which might also lead to fraudulent activities amongst the staff.

5   A risk management group is likely to be headed by the finance director. It also normally includes some other senior accounting staff particularly any staff with experience of fraud or expert knowledge of the accounting system. It is also normal practice to include at least one non finance individual as part of the group.

6   A company's risk appetite is the level of risk that the company is prepared to accept.

7   A fraud response plan is a formal means of setting down the procedures for dealing with any suspected case of misappropriation of assets or falsifying of accounting records.

HOW MUCH HAVE YOU LEARNED? - ANSWERS

Chapter 1 Organisational structure

1   A mission statement is the formal statement of a company's (or other entity's) objectives, business, financial and environmental. In most cases the mission statement will be found as part of the annual financial statements of the company. It may be published on a company's website.

2   (i)   In a vertical structure the tasks of the organisation are grouped into types and each type of task is headed up by a senior manager or director.

   (ii)   In a functional organisation structure there is less emphasis on the personnel in the organisation and more on the actual work functions that are carried out by each area of the business.

   (iii)   A product based organisation chart is where the business is split according to the main types of product of the business rather than according to the various functions that are carried out.

   (iv)   A geographical organisation structure is one where the organisation is split according to the geographical location of its operations.

   (v)   A market sector organisation chart is one where the business is organised around the different market sectors that the business operates in.

3   A management information system is the system within the organisation which allows both internal and external information to be communicated to managers in an appropriate form so that they can carry out their functions as managers.

4   Note that only four types of external stakeholder were required.

   (i)   Shareholders/investors

      The shareholders or investors in a business are the owners of the business whereas the directors are those who are charged with running the business on behalf of them. In large public companies the shareholders will generally have no influence on the general day to day running of the business as this is the job of the directors. However in some instances large institutional investors in particular may be able to bring influence to bear on the practices of the business. This has been seen in recent examples, for example the appointment of a director of Sainsbury plc, who then withdrew at the behest of the institutional shareholder.

   (ii)   Providers of loan finance

      It is often the case that the providers of long term loan finance such as banks or debenture holders will make certain stipulations regarding the practices of the business before being prepared to advance the funds. Therefore it is possible that there may be stipulations regarding the way in which the business is financed in future and the provision of regular management accounts for the provider of the finance.

(iii) Customers

Customers must be provided with the product or service they require, which they perceive to be of the right quality and sold to them at the right price. Therefore as there is increasing emphasis on the quality of goods and services provided to customers this may have a significant affect on how the company is run and organised.

(iv) Suppliers

The suppliers of a business are important stakeholders of the business and a business's relationship with their suppliers and the quality of those supplies is becoming ever more important.

(v) Government

The actions of the Government affect the operations of businesses in many different ways from abiding by Health and Safety regulations, dealing with employment law issues to payment of VAT and PAYE.

(vi) Community

Many businesses feel an obligation to the community in terms of employment and social and environmental responsibilities which have affected the practices of their business.

5 Note that only four external regulations were required.

(i) Companies legislation

The UK Companies Act requires that all limited companies produce annual financial statements for their shareholders, in a certain timescale, in set formats and with detailed disclosure requirements. These regulations affect not only the nature of the accounting records that are kept but also the detailed timing of the production of the financial statements for the year.

(ii) UK accounting regulations

In the UK, Financial Reporting Standards and Statements of Standard Accounting Practice set out the required accounting treatment for all areas of financial reporting and must be followed by limited companies. These accounting standards will therefore affect the type of accounting information that is recorded and the treatment of various items in the company's annual financial statements.

(iii) International accounting regulations

For UK companies, and other European Union companies, there is a move towards international harmonisation of accounting standards and by 2005 many UK companies will be required to produce their annual financial statements in accordance with International Accounting Standards.

(iv)   Auditing regulations

Company law in the UK requires that the annual financial statements for all companies must be audited. Therefore an independent firm of auditors must be employed who will examine the financial statements and prepare a report to the shareholders of the company regarding whether the statements show a true and fair view. Under company law the accounts department staff must provide the auditors with any information that they require in order to carry out the audit and produce the audit report.

(v)   Stock Exchange regulations

For public limited companies whose shares are traded on the Stock Exchange there are further requirements which must be satisfied which will affect accounting procedures and practices. These regulations not only affect matters which must be disclosed in the financial statements but also factors such as the internal controls within the organisation which tend to directly affect the work of the accounting function.

(vi)   Taxation regulations

As well as the annual payment of Corporation Tax the two main areas where accounting procedures will be affected by taxation regulations are for the PAYE system and VAT.

The payroll function will need to ensure that monthly payments are correctly made to the Inland Revenue for PAYE and National Insurance contributions as well as keeping statutory records such as P11s and submitting returns such as P11D and P35 etc.

If a company is registered for VAT then it will normally be required to make a quarterly return to Customs and Excise together with payment of the amount of VAT due for the period.

Both of these types of taxation payments and returns must be produced on time and therefore will not only affect the type of work in the accounting function but also the precise timing of that work.

6   The main purposes of the accounting function are:

- to process the transactions of the business in order to be able to prepare the   annual financial statements and accord with the Companies Act requirements

- to provide relevant and timely information for management

7   (i)   Purchasing

(ii)   Sales

(iii)   Stores

Chapter 2 Planning and coordinating work

1   Corporate objectives are the overall aims of the business and strategies are the means chosen by the directors to achieve those objectives. Budgets in turn are the detailed plans, set out in financial terms, of how those strategies will be carried out.

2 In order of priority:

Urgent and important
Urgent but not important
Non-urgent but important
Non-urgent and unimportant

3
- Financial year end
- Monthly cycle of operations
- Quarterly reporting and payment of VAT
- Monthly reporting and payment of PAYE and NIC

4
- Planning the overall project - you will need to be aware of the start and end time of the project, the tasks that must be completed for the project and the nature of the report that is required

- Scheduling the work - once the tasks for the project are clear then the manager must schedule the work required to ensure that all tasks are completed on time in order to allow subsequent tasks to be carried out and the report to be completed on time

- Allocating the work - the manager must ensure that each task within the project is allocated to the appropriate member of the team

- Coordinate the project activities and resources - the manager must be able to ensure that all tasks are being completed in the correct timescale and that all resources required such as computer time are available as and when required

- Monitoring progress - the project manager will regularly monitor the progress of each team member and their allocated tasks often by daily or weekly project team meetings Where any problems are encountered corrective action must be taken by the project manager

5
- Determine when information when be available and when the draft accounts are required by

- Determine the number of accounts assistants, computer data inputters etc that are available to help in the preparation of the draft accounts

- Determine the order in which the activities involved in preparation of the draft accounts must take place

- Determine realistic time scales for each of those activities

6
- Be prepared to plan for the longer term

- In the shorter term produce a list of tasks for each day

- Prioritise the list and tick off tasks as they are completed

- Have allocated times for employees to see you rather than having an "open door at all times" policy

- Where necessary arrange regular meetings where problems and issues can be aired rather than seeing employees on an ad hoc basis

- Beware of the telephone - do not spend unnecessary amounts of time on telephone calls - be prepared to put the telephone onto divert if necessary

- Beware of e-mail - respond to any incoming e-mails that need your urgent attention but do not be tempted to reply to non-urgent or unimportant e-mails - be prepared to delete e-mails that do not require your attention

- As new tasks appear during the day allocate them to your priority list or delegate

- Try to organise work in batches so that you are working as efficiently as possible

- Ensure that you complete all tasks that you start wherever possible

Chapter 3 Managing a team

1   Matrix management is a system within an organisation where an individual reports to more than one manager on a permanent basis.

2   Tells style - autocratic style where the manager makes all of the decisions and then simply instructs the team who are expected to obey without question.

Sells style - persuasive style where the manager makes all of the decisions but justifies them to the team.

Consults style - the manager consults with the team members and after taking their views into account takes the decisions himself.

Joins style - democratic style where the manager and team members make a decision on the basis of team consensus.

3   The difficulties that managers often face in delegating tasks can be overcome by the following practical measures:

- ensuring that team members are trained so that they are able to carry out the tasks to be delegated to the correct standard

- ensuring that there is full communication between the manager and team members

- ensuring that assistants are fully briefed as to the precise details of the task to be delegated.

4   Principles of good communication include the following:

- whether written or oral communication make sure that the right message gets across - this will often require some planning on the manager's behalf to ensure that he expresses himself fully and clearly - as a manger always ensure that you have the facts right

- ensure that the purpose of the communication is fully understood. Communication can only be effective if the communicator is fully aware of the reason why this communication is taking place - is it to develop plans? is it to monitor and control performance? is it to obtain information?

- the communication should be by an appropriate method and in an appropriate form. Should the communication be in writing or orally? If the communication is to be in writing is it most appropriate as a note or a more formal memo? If the communication is orally should this be face to face or over the telephone, in public or in private?

- if the communication is in writing ensure that it is pitched at the correct level for the person that is being written to - be aware of the knowledge and understanding of the person being written to and where necessary avoid jargon or overly technical terms

- if the communication is oral be aware of non-verbal signals that are part of the communication such as tone of voice, body language, facial expressions etc.

- be aware of the timing of the communication - if information has no immediate use or relevance then it will tend to be ignored or forgotten

- be prepared to listen to any feedback that is prompted by the communication - listening is an underrated skill but very important - listen attentively and actively - ensure that you hear what is being said to you and are not just concentrating on what you are going to say next

5 Ways of creating effective interpersonal relationships include:

- make a good first impression with your appearance, expression, manner, enthusiasm etc

- be aware of other peoples' perceptions of yourself

- try to perceive other people but beware of stereotyping

- be aware of body language - both the body language that you use and that which you perceive in others

- communicate clearly, accurately and with enthusiasm in whatever media of communication you are using

- ensure wherever possible that you put others at ease with your manner and attitude

- listen attentively and actively to others and ensure that you understand what they are saying to you - this may be by the use of open questions which are questions which require an explanation as an answer rather than a "yes" or "no" answer

- try to recognise factors such as bias, ambiguity or distortion of any facts in any information that is being provided to you.

6 Belbin's eight team roles are as follows:

Co-ordinator Effectively runs the team and provides overall coordination

Shaper A motivator and one who spurs others in the team into action

Plant Source of ideas and creativity

Monitor-evaluator The analyst of the team who will analyse the ideas and spot the flaws

Resource-investigator The social element of the team who can find new contacts and respond to a challenge

Implementer The organisational force behind the team concentrating on planning and scheduling

Team worker The diplomat of the team concerned with the maintenance of the team morale

7   The four stages of team development identified by Tuckman were as follows:

Forming stage This is the initial stage where all individuals are getting to know each other, the team objectives are being formed and the various personalities are starting to interact.

Storming stage In this stage the objectives are clarified and this may lead to setting of realistic targets and a degree of trust or might equally see a period of conflict within the team as relationships settle down.

Norming stage At this point the team will be settling down. There will be agreements regarding scheduling of tasks, quality standards and procedures for working.

Performing stage This is the period where the team gets on with its work. Scheduling of tasks will have been agreed and the team project should progress.

8   Factors that should lead to a successful team include the following:

- high level of commitment to team targets and organisational objectives
- effective communication between team members
- good understanding of individuals' roles within the team
- team members taking an active interest in team decisions
- general consensus within the team about decisions
- high levels of job satisfaction amongst team members
- high quality output achieved
- low levels of labour turnover
- low levels of absenteeism.

9   Maslow's hierarchy of needs:

10 Targets should be specific rather than general. Employees will normally respond better to specific targets such as "answering the telephone within three rings" rather than the more general "answering the telephone as quickly as you can".

Standards should be high but attainable. It is generally believed that the setting of a difficult target is more motivating that setting an easily achievable target. However there is a fine line to be drawn here as a high target may stretch an employee to try harder but only if the employee believes that the target is attainable.

The target should be agreed with the employee. Targets or goals will only tend to be motivational if the employee has agreed to the target. If the target has been set by a manager but not agreed with the employee then the goal may simply be ignored by the employee.

Regular feedback should be provided to the employee. If specific, high, attainable and agreed targets are set for an employee's tasks then again they will still only serve to motivate the employee to meet the targets if he is kept informed on a regular basis as to whether or not he is meeting those targets.

11   Extrinsic rewards are rewards that are external to the job itself such as pay, bonuses and working conditions. Intrinsic rewards are those that arise from performing the job itself and job satisfaction. These intrinsic rewards might include meeting deadlines, meeting targets, goals o budgets, producing a good piece of work or meeting quality standards.

Chapter 4 Competence and training

1   Any six of the following:

- carrying out control procedures such as matching of purchase orders to purchase invoice or checking petty cash claims to valid receipts

- writing up books of prime entry such as the cash book and petty cash book

- double entry bookkeeping

- entering transactions into the general ledger and the sales and purchases ledgers

- performing sales or purchase ledger reconciliations

- performing bank reconciliations

- preparing final accounts schedules such as accruals and prepayments and bad and doubtful debts

- preparation of payroll and wages and salaries information

- writing up the fixed asset register

- writing up cost ledger accounts

- preparing budgets

- preparing variance reports

2   Any three of the following:

- Companies Act requirements
- UK accounting standards
- International accounting standards
- taxation regulations
- Stock Exchange requirements

3   The main objectives of a typical staff appraisal scheme include the following:

- performance set by the organisation

- to identify areas for improvement

- to identify areas where training or development are required

- to identify what the employee must do in future in order to play a part in the realisation of departmental or organisational goals

- to set out to the employee the results and standards of performance expected in the next period

- to assess the employee's level of remuneration

- to identify candidates for promotion

- gaining agreement of the employee to the assessment of their past performance and the aims of their future performance and training and development needs.

4   The main stages of a typical staff appraisal scheme are:

Setting the criteria for assesment - Before the assessment of an employee's performance can take place then standards of performance and competencies required for that employee in their role must be determined. This may be based upon the job description for the employee or a job analysis. Only when the standards have been set can the performance of the employee be compared to the standards or required competencies.

Preparing the appraisal report - The next stage is the preparation of the appraisal report which assesses the performance of the employee over the past period. In older style organisations this will tend to be produced by the employee's line manager however there is a growing tendency for the report to be prepared by the employees themselves or by both the employee and the line manager.

Carrying out the appraisal interview - The appraisal interview is the forum for joint discussion of the appraisal report, agreement of areas for improvement, identification of training and development needs and agreement of future actions.

The assessment review - In many systems the actual appraisal and subsequent managerial assessment will be reviewed by a more senior manager.

Preparation of action plan - Once the appraisal has been carried out and reviewed an action plan will be drawn up for the employee which will include plans for future performance standards as well as plans to deal with any training and development needs that were identified in the appraisal review.

Follow up process - This is the very necessary process of monitoring the progress of the action plan and the implementation of any agreed actions by the employee or training agreed by the employer.

5   SMARTER in the context of setting personal development plans means the following:

   S   Specific - the plans that are set must be specific rather than general

   M   Measurable - in order to assess progress in the development plans they should wherever possible be measurable

   A   Agreed - in most cases personal development plans must be agreed with the appropria level of management

   R   Realistic - personal development plans must be realistic in terms of the individual's ski and abilities and the organisation's resources

   T   Time-bounded - wherever possible time scales should be set for individual goals objectives

   E   Evaluated - the personal development plans must be evaluated by the appropriate level management to determine whether they are realistic within the context of the resourc of the organisation

   R   Reviewed - progress towards meeting personal development objectives should reviewed on a regular basis

6   Training needs are the skills and knowledge that an employee needs to carry out his current ro and any immediate future role which he does not at the present time possess. Training nee can be identified from form staff appraisals, from informal monitoring of work and from futu plans for employees.

7   (i)   Internal course unless resources are not available in which case an external course mig be considered

   (ii)   Induction course

   (iii)   Computer based course or possibly external course

   (iv)   External course

Chapter 5 Contingency plans

1   (i)   A contingency is an uncertain event or risk which may or may not happen

   (ii)   A contingency plan is a plan of action if an uncertain, risky event does take place

   (iii)   Contingency planning is the assessment of the probability of a risk or event occurring a of the effect this will have on the business. If the probability is reasonable and the effe material then a plan must be considered to limit the effect if the event were to take plac

2   When planning for contingencies a manager will consider the probability of the risk or eve happening and the effect the risk or event would have on the business. If the probability of t event happening is reasonable but the effect is not material or if the probability is minim despite the effect being material then there will normally be no requirement for a continger plan. However if the probability of the risk or event is reasonable and the effect is likely to material then a contingency plan will normally be put into place.

3 A manager of an accounts department can attempt to identify risks that are not covered by internal controls in the following ways:

- consider problems that the accounting department has had in the past

- communicate with the staff in the accounting department as they may be aware of potential problems that you as a manager are not aware of

- keep up to date with all aspects of the accounting departments work and try to anticipate problems that might occur.

4 The risk of a virus attacking a business's computer system can be limited by the following:

- anti-virus software which will detect and eradicate most viruses before they have a chance to cause any damage

- internal rules regarding the opening of e-mail attachments

- internal rules regarding the downloading of disks which must be checked for viruses before being downloaded

- internal rules regarding the use of unauthorised software in the system.

5 Any three of the following:

- if there is a hardware fault then even with backup data the fault must be diagnosed and corrected before any backup data can be used in the system. The organisation should ensure that it has a maintenance contract with the supplier who can then deal with the fault and put it right

- if data is lost due to a system crash or power cut then regular backup of data will ensure the minimum of losses. However any data that has been lost must be re-input and processed as soon as the fault is dealt with or the power restored. This may mean that overtime has to be worked by all personnel in the accounting function in order to catch up for time lost

- if one part of a system of the computer is corrupted or lost then the remaining computerised elements may continue as normal and all staff must help in reinstating the lost data for that part of the system or take over the normal roles of the employees in that part of the system whilst they reinstate the lost data

- an agreement with a computer bureaux can ensure that their own systems are made available in the event of such an emergency.

6 Contingency plans for staff absences may be required in the following circumstances:

- where a large number of the staff are off sick at any one time, eg when a flu bug hits the accounting department or a case of food poisoning from the same source

- where only a small number of staff are off sick but at a critical period such as the month end or more importantly at the half year or year end

- where staff are unable to come into work for other emergency reasons such as a gas leak in the building or a transport strike.

Chapter 6 Improvements to the accounting system

1   An internal control system can be defined as 'the whole system of controls, financial an
     otherwise, established by the management in order to carry on the business of the enterprise i
     an orderly and efficient manner, ensure adherence to management policies, safeguard th
     assets and secure as far as possible the completeness and accuracy of the records'.

2   ■   Segregation of duties
     ■   Physical controls
     ■   Authorisation and approval
     ■   Management controls
     ■   Supervisory controls
     ■   Organisational controls
     ■   Arithmetical and accounting controls
     ■   Personnel controls

3   The aim of segregation of duties is to ensure wherever possible that one individual cann
     record and process a complete transaction. Wherever possible authorisation, executio
     custody, recording and systems development and daily operations should be carried out I
     different personnel.

4   Examples might include:

     ■   locked petty cash box
     ■   cheques received locked away until banked
     ■   blank cheque books locked in safes
     ■   computer passwords.

5   An internal audit function should be:

     ■   directly accountable to the highest levels of management
     ■   independent and seen to be independent of all levels of management.

6   Examples might include:

     ■   the use of control totals
     ■   checking the arithmetical accuracy of records and data input
     ■   batch totals in a computerised system
     ■   sales ledger, purchase ledger and bank reconciliations
     ■   the use of sales and purchase ledger control accounts
     ■   preparation of trial balances.

7   The main limitations of internal controls are:

     ■   collusion of two or more employees can defeat the aims of segregation of duties a
          facilitate fraudulent activities

     ■   authorisation of controls are only effective if not abused by the person in authority

     ■   managers may override controls for their own purposes.

8   SWOT analysis is analysis which looks at a situation from four perspectives - strengtl
     weaknesses, opportunities and threats. SWOT analysis can be applied to the assessment of

accounting system by considering strengths and weaknesses of the internal control system and internal checks and opportunities and threats that the accounting system faces.

9   Internal customers of the accounts department might include:

- employees paid by the payroll section
- employees claiming petty cash refunds
- line managers
- senior management
- stores function
- sales function.

10   The four stages in the management of quality are:

Stage 1   Set quality standards for each area of the accounting function

Stage 2   Establish procedures and methods of operation to ensure that these quality standards are met

Stage 3   Monitor the actual quality of the service

Stage 4   Take steps to improve the methods of operating to ensure that the quality standards are met

11   The five sets of questions that should be asked when assessing efficiency are:

Step 1 - what?   What is the purpose of the operation?
                        What is being done and why?
                        What else could or should be done?

Step 2 - where?   Where is it being done?
                        Why is it being done there?
                        Where else could or should it be done?

Step 3 - when?   When is it done?
                        Why is it done then?
                        When else could it or should it be done?

Step 4 - who?   Who does it?
                        Why does that person do it?
                        Who else could or should do it?

Step 5 - how?   How is it done?
                        Why is it done that way?
                        How else could it or should it be done?

12 Controllable costs might include:

- stationery costs
- heat, light and power
- overtime costs
- temporary staff costs.

Non-controllable costs might include:

- apportioned costs such as rent
- basic pay of permanent employees
- notional costs such as interest applied to a department.

13 PEST analysis is an analysis of external factors affecting an organisation or part of an organisation under the following four headings:

- Political
- Economic
- Social
- Technological

Examples of factors which may affect an accounting system:

Political	-	changes in company legislation
Economic	-	increase or decrease in sales
Social	-	changing work patterns
Technological	-	technological fraud

Chapter 7 Fraud within the organisation

1 The two main types of fraud that a company might come across are:

- misappropriation of assets
- deliberate misstatement of the financial statements.

2 Any three of the following:

Theft of cash

In most businesses there is always an amount of petty cash which employees with access to may be tempted to steal.

In a retail business with cash in a till there is a much greater temptation to steal. A cashier could fairly easily simply not ring up a sale and take the cash from the customer themselves.

Theft of stock

This is usually small amounts of stock that go missing but are not noticed due to their immaterial nature.

Teeming and lading

Teeming and lading is a common type of fraud within the sales ledger system. It involves stealing of cash or cheques received from customers but it is covered up by the subsequent receipt being set against the original debt and this rolls over until the perpetrator leaves the organisation with the cash in hand or his fraud is detected.

Fictitious employees

This fraud works by a fictitious employee being added to the payroll and the weekly or monthly pay is paid into a bank account in this bogus name with the fraudster collecting the money. This will normally only happen in a large organisation where such an additional employee can go by without being noticed.

Other payroll fraud

Individuals within the organisation can falsify their own time sheets in order to be paid more overtime than they actually worked.

Alternatively a member of the payroll department can deliberately inflate the pay of an individual member of staff to increase their net pay and share in the benefit.

Fictitious suppliers

In this fraud a bogus supplier is set up in the records. Invoices are received from this bogus supplier and company cheques made out to pay the supplier but with the money being collected by the fraudster. For this system to work there would need to be very little segregation of duties in the accounting function or collusion between two or more employees.

Fictitious customer

Here a new, but fictitious, customer is set up and allowed credit. Goods are despatched to the customer but collected by the fraudster. The fictitious customer never pays of course and eventually the debt is written off as bad.

For this to work there will normally have to be collusion between the employee taking customer orders and the employee granting credit to new customers or a situation where one employee is responsible for both roles.

Collusion with customers

This is a system where both the customer and the employee benefit at the business's expense by splitting between them any gains made by the customer. This may be done by an employee in the accounts department charging lower prices on the invoice to the customer than the true value of the goods or by a member of the stores staff under-recording the amount delivered to the customer.

Collusion with suppliers

Here a supplier invoices the business for more goods than were actually received or for a higher value. The supplier is paid the inflated amount and the gain is split between the supplier and the fraudulent employee.

Receipt of invoices for bogus supply of goods or services

The business receives an invoice for supply of goods, or more commonly, services such as consultancy fees. The goods or services were never of course received. The invoice is paid but it is to the account of a fraudulent employee who sent the invoice.

Disposal of assets

In some cases an employee may buy an asset from the business such as a computer or a car for personal use. If the net book value of the asset is manipulated to be lower than the market value, by over-depreciation for example, then the employee will be charged a lower price than the worth of the asset thereby defrauding the business.

Pension funds

Pension funds can be open to misuse for example by the company using pension fund assets or transferring company assets to the pension fund at an over-valued amount.

3   Any three of the following:

Over valuation of stock

This is a method of inflating net assets and profits by over-valuing the closing stock of the business. As this tends to be a subjective area this can be done in a variety of ways:

- pre-year end deliveries to customers or returns to suppliers may be not be recorded

- stock lines may be deliberately miscounted

- obsolete stock may remain in the books at cost rather than being written down to net book value

- individual stock lines may simply be valued at a higher value than their actual cost.

Window dressing

WINDOW DRESSING is the manipulation of events at the year end in order to improve the appearance of the financial statements. Methods include the following:

- over invoicing before the year end and issuing credit notes after the year end

- not recording purchases of goods just before the year end until after the year end

- deliberately not paying suppliers before the year end in order to increase the cash balance or decrease the overdraft

Not writing off bad debts

Any long-standing bad debts should be written off but by not doing so the asset base of the company is over-stated and the profit is greater.

Manipulation of depreciation charges

If depreciation rates which are lower than they should be are applied to the fixed assets then this will lead to a higher net book value and higher profits than if the true depreciation rate were used.

Fictitious sales

Invoicing bogus customers before the year end and then sending out credit notes after the year end or writing off the debt after the year end will increase profits and debtors for the current year.

Understating expenses

If expenses are omitted from the financial records or accruals not accounted for at the year end this will overstate both profits and net assets.

4   Any three of the following:

Corporate culture

The attitude within an organisation, or its corporate culture, can play a large part in whether it is a high or low risk environment for fraud. A culture where small unethical practices such as stealing of stationery or false expense claims are tolerated may in turn lead to larger frauds by employees or higher levels of management. If a company has a clear anti-fraud policy then this may lead to a culture within the organisation which does not tolerate fraud of any size or at any level.

Size and organisation structure

A large organisation can sometimes be more likely to suffer fraudulent activities as it is easier for employees to be anonymous and for transactions to get lost. Equally if there is a complex organisation structure then this may increase the likelihood of fraud.

However in a small organisation there will tend to be a lack of segregation of duties and this again can facilitate fraud.

A lack of management supervision or a lack of clear management control of responsibility, authority and delegation may also be indicative of a potential for fraudulent activities.

Changes in profit levels

If profit levels show a decrease and appear to be suddenly significantly lower than competitors then this may be an indication of the misappropriation of assets or possibly of deliberate misstatement of the financial statements.

If profit levels suddenly increase, or sales rise without a proportionate increase in costs then this may be evidence of the creation of fictitious customers, collusion with customers or manipulation of the financial statements.

Individual employee's behaviour

Few people are brazen enough to carry out fraud without there being some hint of this in their behaviour. Some employees may become excessively secretive about their duties at work whereas others involved in fraud may become irritable if anyone questions them, however innocently, about their tasks or role. As a manager you should be alert to unusual, irrational or inconsistent behaviour.

Excessive hours

If an employee is perpetrating a fraud then they run the risk of it being discovered if anyone else carries out their tasks even for a short period of time. Therefore employees who work excessively long hours, refuse to take holidays or insist that certain tasks should not be carried out until they return from holiday may potentially be involved in fraudulent activities.

Expensive lifestyle

This is one of the most common indicators of fraud. An employee suddenly appears to be livin
a lifestyle which would normally be beyond their means - cars, holidays, moving house etc
Such things may be flaunted at work and excuses such as a sudden inheritance given but, as
manager, it may put you on your guard.

Management style

Detecting fraud can be extremely difficult when it is being perpetrated by a senior member o
the management team or a director. If such a person has an autocratic management style, wid
ranging powers, a dominant personality and is very senior in the organisation it is the rare, lowe
level manager or employee who will question his actions and their fraudulent activities ca
carry on for a considerable period of time without being detected.

Staff problems

Another common cause of individual employees carrying out fraudulent activities is if they be
a grudge against their employer. If employees feel that they are not sufficiently remunerated
they have been passed over for promotion this can be a strong motive for an individual with th
opportunity to commit a fraud.

An environment where there are dissatisfied staff, low salary levels for key staff, person
financial pressures on key staff or potential labour force reductions or redundancies, may b
much more susceptible to fraud.

Targets and budgets

In many organisations the overall remuneration of managers and key employees may b
dependent upon their meeting high or aggressive targets or budget figures. Where manageme
compensation is highly dependent upon meeting such targets there may be temptation
manipulate the financial accounting figures in order to appear to meet such targets.

Administration issues

Some fairly simple administrative issues may be indicators of a possible fraud. If documents a
records are being frequently altered or there is extensive use of correction fluid or t
production of photocopies of documents rather than originals these may be indicators t
something is wrong. Other potential indicators might be stamps rather than original signatur
signature or handwriting discrepancies or transactions which are taking place without t
appropriate authorisation.

Accounting problems

As we saw in the previous chapter there will be many internal checks built into the inter
control system designed to find errors or potential frauds. If these checks highlight proble
then this may be an indicator of fraud. For example, control accounts which cannot
reconciled, unreconciling bank reconciliations, unexplained stock adjustments or confirmat
letters not returned from suppliers or customers.

5   There are a variety of stages in this risk assessment with regard to fraud:

   ■   establish a risk management group
   ■   identify risk areas
   ■   analyse fraud risks
   ■   assess the scale of risk
   ■   develop and implement a risk management strategy.

6   The main risk areas in the accounting system are:

   ■   the sales cycle
   ■   the purchases cycle
   ■   the payroll cycle
   ■   cash payments
   ■   cash receipts
   ■   expenses
   ■   stock
   ■   fixed assets.

7   A risk management group is a group of normally senior employees whose tasks is to review the risks of fraud that the organisation faces. Its responsibilities are to review the systems and procedures for weaknesses, identify and assess any risks and introduce relevant controls to deal with these risks.

8   The fraud officer is a senior member of the management of an organisation with the following roles:

   ■   to receive information from staff confidentially
   ■   to provide advice to individuals with suspicions
   ■   to implement the fraud response plan
   ■   to initiate and oversee any fraud investigations
   ■   to liase with any third parties as necessary
   ■   to carry out any required follow up actions.

REVISION COMPANION

chapter 1:
ORGANISATIONAL STRUCTURE

Explain what is meant by a company's mission statement.

Briefly describe four different types of organisational structure.

What are the three main roles of managers?

Describe four external stakeholders in a business and the possible effect they might have on the organisation and procedures of the business.

Describe four types of external regulations and the effect they may have on the accounting practices and functions of the business.

What other internal functions in a manufacturing company might the accounting function find that it has a relationship with?

What are the main resources required by the accounting function?

Chapter 2:
PLANNING AND CO-ORDINATING WORK

Distinguish between the objectives and the strategies of a business. Give an example of an objective and a strategy for a business.

The tasks that the accounts personnel have to be carried out have been classified as follows:

a) urgent but not important

b) not urgent but important

c) not urgent and not important

d) urgent and important

In what order should these four categories of tasks be carried out?

Explain the importance of meeting deadlines and why it is important that any possible failure to meet a deadline should be reported as soon as possible.

Briefly explain four external timescales that a business might face.

What are the typical roles of a project manager?

What are the main activities for a manager involved in scheduling a job or project?

Describe the general principles of good time management.

chapter 3:
MANAGING A TEAM

What is meant by a matrix management system?

Distinguish between the roles of a manager and of a supervisor.

Briefly explain the four Ashridge management styles (tells, sells, consults, joins).

In practice why do some managers find it difficult to delegate work and how can these difficulties be overcome?

What are the main methods of creating effective interpersonal relationships in the workplace?

Distinguish between a multi disciplinary team and a multi skilled team.

Briefly explain Maslow's hierarchy of needs and how this effects the motivation of employees.

In Herzberg's motivation theory what are hygiene factors and motivator factors?

chapter 4:
COMPETENCE AND TRAINING

As a manager in an accounts department what type of skills and knowledge might you look for in your assistants?

What are the objectives of a staff appraisal scheme?

What are the stages in a staff appraisal process?

If you were considering a personal development plan and were making it a SMARTER plan what factors would you include in the plan?

What are the typical methods of training available to employees in a company?

What are the typical procedures that take place during induction training?

7   What would be the most appropriate method of training in each of the following circumstances?

(i)   New Health and Safety regulations have been introduced which affect the company and all employees need to know about them.

(ii)   One of the senior sales ledger clerks is due to go on maternity leave and her responsibility for the month end sales ledger control account reconciliation is due to pass to a junior sales ledger clerk who has never performed the reconciliation before.

(iii)   A new member of the accounts department is struggling with her basic double entry bookkeeping but she does not wish to obtain any professional qualifications such as AAT.

(iv)   An employee has recently qualified as an AAT Technician and wishes to move on to study for the ICAEW qualification.

chapter 5:
CONTINGENCY PLANS

Define a contingency and a contingency plan.

What are the two elements to consider about uncertain events when contingency planning?

What possible contingency plan might there be for a computer system crash?

Give examples of both predictable and unpredictable staff absences.

What are the advantages of multi skilled employees within an accounts department?

Chapter 6:
IMPROVEMENTS TO THE ACCOUNTING SYSTEM

What is an internal control system and what are its main aims?

Distinguish between administrative internal controls and accounting internal controls.

What are the eight general internal controls appearing in the mnemonic SPAM SOAP?

What are the two most important features of an internal audit function?

Give four examples of arithmetical or accounting controls.

What are internal checks and what are their main purposes?

What is a SWOT analysis within an accounting system?

What are the four stages in the management of quality in the accounting function?

What is meant by effectiveness and cost-effectiveness within the accounting function?

What is a PEST analysis? Give an example for each of the factors in a PEST analysis which might affect the operations of the accounting function.

Chapter 7:
FRAUD WITHIN THE
ORGANISATION

What is teeming and lading?

How would a fraud involving a fictitious supplier work?

How could sales ledger personnel defraud their company by collusion with a customer?

What effect would the over-valuation of stock at the year end have on the financial statements and how could this over-valuation take place?

Note down as many common indicators of fraudulent activity as you can think of.

What is a Risk Management Group? What is its role within a company? Which personnel should normally be part of a Risk Management Group?

What is a fraud response plan?

What are the main duties of a fraud officer in a company?

ANSWERS TO REVISION COMPANION ACTIVITIES

A company's mission statement is a statement of its overall aims and objectives. This will tend to cover all aspects of the company aims not just financial and business objectives but also social and environmental.

Any four of the following:

a) Vertical structure - in a vertical structure the tasks of the organisation are grouped into types and each type of task is headed up by a senior manager or director.

b) Functional structure - in a functional organisation structure there is less emphasis on the personnel in the organisation and more on the actual work functions that are carried out by each area of the business. Therefore each function such as marketing, production, stores, accounting etc would be a separate area of the business.

c) Product structure - many organisations produce a variety of different products which may be very diverse and in such organisations the structure is often based about those product groups.

d) Geographical structure - some organisations may find that the most sensible structure is that based upon the geographical activities of the business. For example a wholesaler with operations in a number of parts of the country may have regional managers for each area who all report to the Managing Director at the Head Office.

e) Market sector structure - in some organisations the sales that are made are to very different sectors of the market although they may be similar products. This will affect the way in which the organisation operates and the structure may reflect these market sectors. Operations will be structured around each market sector that the business operates in.

The three main roles of managers are planning, decision making and control.

Any four of the following:

a) Shareholders or investors - the shareholders of a company are the owners of the company and the people on behalf of whom the managers and directors run the company. In some small private companies the directors will also be the shareholders and therefore the direction which the company takes will be largely determined internally. However in larger public companies the shareholders may be institutional investors, venture capital firms or individual private investors.

In such cases the aims of the directors, in the form of the mission statement and strategies may not always be the same as those of the main shareholders in the company. In some case the direction of the company may be heavily influenced by the requirements of the mai shareholders, particularly institutional investors and venture capitalists.

b)   Providers of loan finance - most companies will be financed not just by ordinary share capita but also by a variety of types of short or long term debt finance. The providers of such financ will have an interest in not only the profitability of the company but also in the security of th debt. The requirements of these stakeholders may therefore influence the manner in whic the company operates.

- Loan finance may take the form of:
- long term bank lending
- bank overdraft finance
- debenture loans
- lease finance

In the case of the first three of these types of loan finance the provider of the finance ma specify how the company is financed in the future and may also require regular financial an management accounting updates in order to assess the security of their loans.

c)   Customers - if a company is to remain in business in the long term then it must satisfy i customers. This means that customers must be provided with the product or service the require, which they perceive to be of the right quality and sold to them at the right pric There is an increasing emphasis on the quality of goods and services provided to custome with many companies moving towards Total Quality Management which has a significa effect on how the company is run and organised.

d)   Suppliers - the suppliers of a business are important stakeholders of the business. / businesses move towards Total Quality Management and Just in time purchasing the relationship with their suppliers and the quality of those supplies becomes ever mo important.

e)   Government - the actions of the Government affect the operations of businesses in ma different ways from abiding by Health and Safety regulations, dealing with employment la issues to payment of VAT and PAYE.

f)   The community - in recent years there has been increasing pressure upon companies to a in the interests of the community and general environment as well as to make profits. Th emphasis on social and environmental factors has forced changes in outlook in ma businesses with mission statements reflecting not just the commercial aims of the organisatic but also its social and environmental responsibilities.

5   Any four of the following:

a)   Legal requirements - the UK Companies Act requires that all limited companies produ annual financial statements for their shareholders, in a certain timescale, in set formats a with detailed disclosure requirements. These regulations affect not only the nature of t accounting records that are kept but also the detailed timing of the production of the financ statements for the year.

b)   UK accounting regulations - in the UK the accounting profession produces   Financ Reporting Standards (FRSs), set by the Accounting Standards Board. These FRSs and sor older Statements of Standard Accounting Practice (SSAPs) set out the required accounting treatment for all areas of financial reporting and must be followed by limited companies. These accounting standards will therefore affect the type of accounting information that is recorded and the treatment of various items in the company's annual financial statements.

c)   International accounting regulations - the International Accounting Standards Committee also produces International Accounting Standards (IASs) and International Financial Reporting Standards (IFRSs). The importance of these for UK companies is that there is a move towards international harmonisation of accounting standards and by 2005 many UK companies will be required to produce their annual financial statements in accordance with International Accounting Standards.

d)   Auditing regulations - Company law in the UK requires that the annual financial statements for all companies must be audited. An audit is an independent examination of the financial statements with the outcome of an expression of opinion on whether those statements present a 'true and fair view' and whether they comply with the Companies Act. In practice this means that an independent firm of auditors must be employed who will examine the financial statements and prepare a report to the shareholders of the company regarding whether the statements show a true and fair view.

Under company law the accounts department staff must provide the auditors with any information that they require in order to carry out the audit and produce the audit report.

e)   Stock Exchange Regulations - for public limited companies whose shares are traded on the Stock Exchange there are further requirements which must be satisfied which will affect accounting procedures and practices. These regulations not only affect matters which must be disclosed in the financial statements but also factors such as the internal controls within the organisation which tend to directly affect the work of the accounting function.

f)   Taxation regulations - as well as the annual payment of Corporation Tax the two main areas where accounting procedures will be affected by taxation regulations are for the PAYE system and VAT. The payroll function will need to ensure that monthly payments are correctly made to the Inland Revenue for PAYE and National Insurance contributions as well as keeping statutory records such as P11s and submitting returns such as P11D and P35 etc. If a company is registered for VAT then it will normally be required to make a quarterly return to Customs and Excise together with payment of the amount of VAT due for the period.

Both of these types of taxation payments and returns must be produced on time and therefore will not only affect the type of work in the accounting function but also the precise timing of that work.

In a manufacturing organisation the accounting function is likely to have relationships with the following other functions in the organisation:

a)   Purchasing - many manufacturing organisations will have a separate purchasing function. This department will send purchase orders to suppliers on the basis of requisitions from other functions such as the stores department or factory floor. The purchase order will then be sent to the accounting function to be matched with the supplier's invoice when it arrives.

b)   Stores - the stores department will not only often raise a purchase requisition for materials or goods required but will also fill out a Goods Received Note (GRN) to evidence the receipt of the goods. The GRN will also be sent to the accounting function to be matched with the purchase order and eventual receipt of the supplier's invoice.

In some organisations it may also be the case that the sales department contacts the store function with details of customer orders. The stores function then despatches the goods an sends the despatch note to the accounting function in order for an invoice to be produced

c) Sales - in many organisations there will be a separate sales function which liaises wi customers and takes customer orders. The sales invoice will then either be raised by the sal function or the details will be sent to the accounting function for them to raise the invoic The accounting function will of course have to record the invoice in the sales ledger ar general ledger and also monitor receipt of payment from the customer.

d) Production - in a manufacturing organisation it is likely that the production or manufacturir area of the organisation will need costing information. The accounting function will I expected to provide such information.

7   The main resources required by an accounting function are:

People - it must be properly staffed with the required number of staff with the required skills ar qualifications.

Materials - such as adequate supplies of pre-printed stationery such as sales invoices and cre notes and items such as paper clips, staples, calculators

Equipment - the type of equipment required for the accounting function will largely be des chairs, filing cabinets, safes and computers.

Information - the accounting function will require information from a number of other sourc within the organisation - sales details from the sales department, purchases details from t purchasing department, stock movement details from the stores department, production deta from the factory etc.

Chapter 2:
PLANNING AND CO-ORDINATING WORK

The objectives of a business are its overall aims or where it wants to be in the future. The strategies of a business are the methods by which the business will achieve its objectives.

A business may have an objective of increasing the quality of its products without price increases. The strategies to achieve this might include just in time purchasing, introduction of total quality management or value added analysis.

i)   urgent and important
ii)   urgent but not important
iii)   not urgent but important
iv)   not urgent and not important

It is important to meet any deadlines that have been set as the work of other individuals or departments of the business may be dependent upon this particular deadline being met. If it becomes clear that it is possible that a deadline might not be met then this should be reported to the appropriate person as soon as possible not only so that any potential work disruption due to the failure to meet the deadline can be dealt with but also as managers may be able to free up resources that mean that the original deadline can in fact be met.

Four external timescales that a business might face might include the following:

a)   the financial year end - this will require a trial balance at the year end, a variety of reconciliations and eventually preparation of the financial statements

b)   quarterly reporting for VAT - each quarter the VAT return must be completed on time and returned, together with payment, to Customs and Excise

c)   monthly reporting to the Inland Revenue- each month the amounts due to the Inland Revenue for PAYE and National Insurance must be paid

d)   monthly operating cycles- in many accounting departments the month end will see an increase in activity due to sending out of customer statements, preparation of bank reconciliations, reconciliation of suppliers' statements etc.

The typical roles of a project manager include the following:

- planning the project
- scheduling the work involved
- allocating the work to appropriate members of the team

- coordinating the project activities and
- monitoring the progress of the project.

6   The main activities for a manager involved in scheduling a job or project include the following:

- determining the start and completion time of the project
- determining the resources available (people/computer time etc)
- determining the order in which activities must take place
- determining realistic time scales for each activity
- allocating each activity to the appropriate person
- coordinating the work of each individual
- reviewing the schedule and dealing with unexpected events.

7   The general principles of good time management include the following:

- break down your overall job into its specific tasks so that you know precisely what your wo⬛ goals are

- make plans setting out in detail how you will achieve those goals - the tasks, timescale⬛ deadlines, resources required etc

- make lists at the start of each week and at the start of each day of the precise tasks that nee⬛ to be completed each day. Once a task is completed tick it off the list. If a task cannot ⬛ completed in a day add it to the list for the following day

- set your priorities detailing which tasks are the ones that must be completed first and which c⬛ be left for later

- concentrate, wherever possible, on trying to complete one task at a time once you have start⬛ it. There will be occasions where a task cannot be completed at that particular time and m⬛ be added to the next day's list but try to keep these to a minimum

- do not put off large, difficult or uninteresting tasks but make sure that you do them now and ⬛ not have to add them to tomorrow's list.

hapter 3:
MANAGING A TEAM

Matrix management is a system within an organisation where an individual reports to more than one manager on a permanent basis.

A supervisor's role will tend to be different from that of a manager in the following ways:

- only a limited amount of a supervisor's time is spent on management responsibilities

- most of a supervisor's time is spent doing his actual job

- the employees reporting to the supervisor will be non-managerial employees

- the supervisor will concentrate on day to day operations

- the supervisor will require detailed and frequent information in order to be able to plan and control the operations for which he or she is responsible.

The four Ashridge management styles are:

Tells - this style, also known as the autocratic style, occurs when the manager makes all of the decisions and then simply instructs the team who are expected to obey without question.

Sells - also known as the persuasive style, this involves the manager making all of the decisions but in this style of leadership the manager believes that the team members must be motivated to work properly and efficiently and therefore he or she sells or justifies the decisions to his or her team.

Consults - this is a less autocratic style and is where the manager consults with team members but after taking their views into account finally takes the decisions himself.

Joins - also known as the democratic style, this is where the manager and the team members make a decision on the basis of team consensus.

Some managers often find it difficult to delegate work to more junior staff for the following reasons:

- lack of faith in the ability of assistants to carry out the task to the manager's standards

- concern about the effects of mistakes by assistants and the costs of putting those mistakes right

- a need to stay in touch with the workings of the team by carrying out tasks that could be delegated

However there are ways of overcoming these reasons for not delegating and they include:

- ensuring that team members are trained in such a way as to be able to carry out the tasks th are delegated to the correct quality standards

- ensuring that there is full communication in both directions between the manager and th assistant as this will increase the confidence of the manager and the assistant alike

- ensuring that the assistant is fully briefed as to the precise details of the task that is to t carried out.

5   The main methods of creating effective interpersonal relationships in the workplace include th following:

- make a good first impression with your appearance, expression, manner, enthusiasm etc

- be aware of other peoples' perceptions of yourself

- try to perceive other people but beware of stereotyping

- be aware of body language - both the body language that you use and that which yc perceive in others

- communicate clearly, accurately and with enthusiasm in whatever medium of communicatic you are using

- ensure wherever possible that you put others at ease with your manner and attitude

- listen attentively and actively to others and ensure that you understand what they are sayi to you - this may be by the use of open questions which are questions which require explanation as an answer rather than a 'yes' or 'no' answer

- try to recognise factors such as bias, ambiguity or distortion of any facts in any informati that is being provided to you.

6   A multi disciplinary team is a team in which the members have different specialisms such marketing and design as well as accounting. In such a team the skills, knowledge and experien of the team members are all exchanged.

A multi skilled team is a team where each individual has a number of skills and can each perfo any of the tasks that the team has to perform.

Maslow argues that individuals have a number of basic needs. These start from basic physiological needs such as food and shelter and then progress upwards through a hierarchy as follows:

His theory is that individuals will be motivated by each of these needs from the bottom of the hierarchy to the top. Once a need has been fully satisfied however it is no longer a motivating factor.

Physiological needs are the basic factors of food and shelter.

Once the need for food and shelter is satisfied, individuals then move on to require security, freedom from threats and a feeling of general order, which are safety needs.

Love/social needs are those which need to be satisfied after the basic safety needs have been met, whereby individuals will be looking for relationships and affection and within a work and social context a feeling of belonging.

Esteem needs are the higher level needs are perhaps most relevant to the work environment and relate to recognition, respect and status.

Finally self-actualisation, once all other needs have been satisfied, is the motivating factor for individuals wanting fulfilment of their own personal potential.

According to Herzberg hygiene factors are the conditions of work such as pay, working conditions, job security, company policy, administration, quality of supervision etc. Such factors will tend not to actually motivate employees but if they are poor or inadequate then they can cause dissatisfaction and be demotivating factors.

Motivating factors are factors which affect personal growth and which do in fact create job satisfaction and motivate individuals to perform more effectively. Motivator factors include responsibility, challenges, achievement, status, promotion, recognition and personal growth in the job.

Chapter 4:
COMPETENCE AND TRAINING

The types of skills and knowledge that a manager in an accounts department would be looking for in his assistants would be:

- technical skills
- professional knowledge
- administrative skills
- computer skills
- interpersonal skills

The objectives of a typical staff appraisal scheme include the following:

- to review the performance of the employee and compare to standards of performance set by the organisation

- to identify areas for improvement

- to identify areas where training or development are required

- to identify what the employee must do in future in order to play a part in the realisation of departmental or organisational goals

- to set out to the employee the results and standards of performance expected in the next period

- to assess the employee's level of remuneration

- to identify candidates for promotion

- gaining agreement of the employee to the assessment of their past performance and the aims of their future performance and training and development needs.

The stages in a staff appraisal process are:

a) Setting the criteria for assessment - before the assessment of an employee's performance can take place standards of performance and competencies required for that employee in their role must be determined.

b) Appraisal report - in this next stage the appraisal report assesses the performance of the employee over the past period.

    c)   Appraisal interview - this is the forum for joint discussion of the appraisal report, agreemen of areas for improvement, identification of training and development needs and agreemen of future actions.

    d)   Assessment review - in many systems the actual appraisal and subsequent manageri assessment will be reviewed by a more senior manager.

    e)   Action plan - once the appraisal has been carried out and reviewed an action plan will k drawn up for the employee which will include plans for future performance standards as we as plans to deal with any training and development needs that were identified in the apprais review.

    f)   Follow up - this is the very necessary process of monitoring the progress of the action pl and the implementation of any agreed actions by the employee or training agreed by th employer.

4   When considering a personal development plan it is advised that it should be SMARTER. Th means that the following factors should be included:

- the plan should be specific rather than general with particular goals and aims
- the goals and aims should be measurable
- the goals and aims should be agreed with the relevant mangers
- the goals and aims should be realistic
- there should be a time limit set on the goals and aims
- the plan must be evaluated by the appropriate management for its feasibility
- the plan must be reviewed at regular intervals to ensure that it is on target.

5   The typical methods of training available are :

- induction training
- on the job training
- training courses
- computer based training
- mentoring.

6   The typical procedures that take place during induction training are:

- explanation of the hours of work, lunch breaks etc

- explanation of the requirements of the new employee's job and the goals of each task

- explanation of the aims and goals of the department as a whole

- introduction to fellow employees and particularly any supervisor to whom the employee v be reporting

- explanation of the overall structure of the department

- introduction to machinery that may be used as part of the job such as computer termin printers, photocopiers etc

- introduction to the health and safety policy of the organisation and explanation of who health and safety officer is

- assessment of any detailed training that the employee will require in order to carry out his job - this may include on the job training, formal training courses or mentoring

- organisation of training programme for new employee.

i)   Internal training course
ii) On the job training
iii) External double entry bookkeeping course or home study
iv) External professional training course

chapter 5:
CONTINGENCY PLANS

A contingency is a risk which may or may not happen. A contingency plan is a plan of how to deal with a risk that is recognised but by its nature is possible although unlikely.

The two elements to consider are:

- the probability of the event happening
- the level of impact of the event on the business

Regular backup of data will ensure the minimum of losses in a computer system crash. However any data that has been lost must be re- input and processed as soon as the fault is dealt with. This may mean that overtime has to be worked by all personnel in the accounting function in order to catch up for time lost.

Predictable staff absences include holidays, study leave and maternity leave. Unpredictable staff absences are mainly due to sickness or unexpected resignations.

Multi skilled employees are those that can carry out a number of different tasks within their department not just the tasks that they deal with on a normal daily basis. In an accounts department there will be many tasks that must be carried out such as writing up the various day books, carrying out reconciliations, dealing with petty cash or the payroll. The advantage of multi skilled employees is that they are able to cover the tasks of other absent employees whether this absence is temporary due to illness or more permanent due to resignation or promotion.

chapter 6:
IMPROVEMENTS TO THE
ACCOUNTING SYSTEM

An internal control system can be defined as 'the whole system of controls, financial and otherwise, established by the management in order to carry on the business of the enterprise in an orderly and efficient manner, ensure adherence to management policies, safeguard the assets and secure as far as possible the completeness and accuracy of the records'.

The aims of such a system of internal control are as follows:

- efficiency of the operations

- adherence to management policies

- safeguard the assets of the business

- ensure completeness and accuracy of the accounting records

Administrative internal controls are the methods and procedures in the business which are concerned with the operational efficiency of the business and adherence to management policies.

Accounting internal controls are the methods and procedures that are concerned with safeguarding the assets of the business and ensuring the completeness, accuracy and reliability of the financial records.

The eight general internal controls are:

Segregation of duties
Physical
Authorisation and approval
Management

Supervision
Organisation
Arithmetical and accounting
Personnel

4   The two most important features of an internal audit function are:

- that it is and is seen to be independent of management influence

- that it reports to the highest level of management, usually the Board of Directors or the Audit Committee.

5   Any four of:

- pre-lists
- post-lists
- batch totals
- control totals
- control account reconciliations for sales ledger or purchase ledger
- bank reconciliations
- trial balances.

6   Internal checks are a part of the internal control system which provide checks on the day-to-day transactions which are part of the routine system where the work of one person is independently checked by another or is complementary to the work of another.

The main purposes of internal checks are:

- to break down procedures into separate steps
- to segregate tasks so that responsibility for a task or transaction can be traced to an individual
- to keep the records of control totals etc as evidence of the accuracy of the accounting
- to reduce the possibility of fraud or error.

7   A SWOT analysis is an analysis of the strengths, weaknesses, opportunities and threats which affect each element of the accounting system.

8   The four stages in the management of quality in the accounting function are:

Stage 1 Set quality standards for each area of the accounting function

Stage 2 Establish procedures and methods of operation to ensure that these quality standards are met

Stage 3 Monitor the actual quality of the service

Stage 4 Take steps to improve the methods of operating to ensure that the quality standards a met.

9   Effectiveness can be described as the means of achieving the desired objective. Cost-effectiveness is achieving that objective at the minimum cost level. The work of the accounting function should be carried out at the required quality level in order to meet the department's objectives but at the lowest possible cost.

10 A PEST analysis is an analysis of the external factors affecting the accounting system under the headings of:

Political factors
Economic factors
Social factors
Technological factors

Examples of each these factors which might affect the operations of the accounting function include:

Political factors:

- changes in NIC rates
- changes in VAT rates
- changes in company legislation regarding publication of financial statements
- changes in Financial Reporting Standards

Economic factors:

- increase/decrease in volume of transactions due to general or specific changes in the economy and customer demands

- changes in the availability and wage rates of the labour force

- the staff available to work in the accounting function

- the budget applied to the accounting function

Social factors:

- changing work patterns such as flexitime and home working
- family commitments leading to changes such as part time working or job sharing
- employment legislation

Technological factors:

- advances in computer systems
- security issues
- technological fraud
- on-line banking

Chapter 7:
FRAUD WITHIN THE
ORGANISATION

Teeming and lading is a common type of fraud within the sales ledger system. It involves stealing of cash or cheques received from customers but it is covered up by the subsequent receipts being set against the original debt and this rolls over until the perpetrator leaves the organisation with the cash in hand or his fraud is detected.

Fraud involving a fictitious supplier starts with the details of the bogus supplier being entered into the accounting records. Invoices are received from this bogus supplier and company cheques made out to pay the supplier but with the money being collected by the fraudster.

By colluding with a customer it is possible for sales ledger personnel to defraud their company whilst both the customer and the sales ledger employee benefit by splitting between them any gains made by the customer. This may be done by sales ledger personnel charging lower prices on the invoice to the customer than the true value of the goods or by under-recording the amount delivered to the customer. The customer therefore pays less for the goods received than they were worth and splits the difference with the sales ledger employee.

Over-valuation of stock at the year end means that closing stock is over valued and therefore the recorded profit and the net asset value of the company are both over stated.

Over-valuation of stock can be achieved in a variety of ways:

- pre-year end deliveries to customers or returns to suppliers may not be recorded

- stock lines may be deliberately miscounted

- obsolete stock may remain in the books at cost rather than being written down to net book value

- individual stock lines may simply be valued at a higher value than their actual cost.

5 Common indicators of fraud might include the following:

- a corporate culture which is not specifically anti-fraud
- a large or complex organisation structure
- sudden changes in profit levels
- erratic or suspicious individual employee's behaviour
- excessive hours worked by an individual employee
- expensive lifestyle of an employee
- autocratic management style
- staff problems such as disgruntled employees or imminent redundancies
- targets and budgets set too high to meet
- administration issues
- accounting problems

6 A Risk Management Group is a group of fairly senior management which is established to conduc a review of the risks of fraud that the organisation faces and to be responsible for reviewing system and procedures, identifying and assessing risks and introducing controls best suited to the situatior The group will need to assess the organisation's risk appetite which is the level of risk that th organisation is prepared to accept, and recommend and implement changes to systems an procedures where the risk of fraud in an area of the accounting system exceeds this risk appetit level.

The members of the Risk Management Group should be individuals with expertise in th company's systems and procedures, a basic knowledge of fraud and the knowledge and authorit to introduce changes to procedures and new controls. This is likely to include the finance directc other senior accounting personnel and normally at least one non-finance individual to bring different perspective to the group.

7 A fraud response plan is a formal means of setting down the procedures for dealing with ar suspected case of theft, misappropriation of assets or falsifying of accounting records. Such a pla can also be of use as a deterrent to fraud and giving employees more confidence to come forwar if any form of fraud is suspected. The fraud response plan is the means by which the organisatior attitude to fraud is communicated to all employees, managers, directors and even shareholders.

8 The main duties of a fraud officer within a company are:

- to receive information from staff confidentially and if necessary anonymously
- to provide advice to individuals who report suspicions of fraudulent activities
- to implement the fraud response plan
- to be responsible for initiating and overseeing any fraud investigations
- to liase with any third parties where necessary
- to carry out any further follow up actions

AAT

SAMPLE SIMULATION
UNIT 10

MANAGING PEOPLE AND SYSTEMS AND PEOPLE IN THE ACCOUNTING ENVIRONMENT

AAT CASE STUDY: MANAGING SYSTEMS AND PEOPLE IN THE ACCOUNTING ENVIRONMENT

DELMAR ELECTRONICS LTD.

LES NIGHTINGALE

CONTENTS

This case study is designed for candidates to be able to use, in order to demonstrate their competence in managing systems and people in the accounting environment.

PERFORMANCE CRITERIA FOR THIS UNIT

All performance criteria for this unit **must** be covered in the project report based on this case study, or by other documented evidence.

Element	PC Coverage

10.1   Manage people within the accounting environment

A   Plan work activities to make the optimum use of resources and to ensure that work is completed within agreed timescales.

B   Review the competence of individuals undertaking work activities and arrange the necessary training.

C   Prepare, in collaboration with management, contingency plans to meet possible emergencies.

D   Communicate work methods and schedules to colleagues in ways that help them understand what is expected of them.

E   Monitor work activities closely to ensure that quality standards are being met.

F	Co-ordinate work activities effectively and in accordance with work plans and contingency plans.

G	Encourage colleagues to report to you promptly any problems and queries that are beyond their authority or expertise to resolve, and resolve these where they are within your authority and expertise.

H	Refer problems and queries to the appropriate person where resolution is beyond your authority or expertise.

10.2 Identify opportunities for improving the effectiveness of an accounting system

A	Identify weaknesses and potential for improvement to the accounting system and consider their impact on the operation of the organisation.

B	Identify potential areas of fraud arising from control avoidance within the accounting system and grade the risk.

C	Review methods of operating regularly in respect of their cost-effectiveness, reliability and speed.

D	Make recommendations to the appropriate person in a clear, easily understood format.

E	Ensure recommendations are supported by a clear rationale which includes an explanation of any assumptions made.

F	Update the system in accordance with changes that affect the way the system should operate and check that your update is producing the required results.

THE DEL CASE STUDY

THE COMPANY'S BACKGROUND AND MANAGEMENT

It is now April 2003. Your name is Tony Bush, and you are employed as an accounting systems technician with Delmar Electronics Limited (DEL).

The company was established six years ago by three colleagues, Richard West, Omar Sangha and John Bryce, who all knew each other well from working together in the electronics sector. Richard and Omar were both working at the time for Fort Technology Plc, a large quoted manufacturer of semi conductor testing equipment. Richard was the technical director and Omar a technical sales manager. John Bryce was employed as production manager in a similar electronics manufacturing company.

Four years ago Elaine Candler joined DEL as finance director, the fourth member of the board.

Their current positions in DEL are:

Richard West	**Managing Director**
Elaine Candler	**Finance Director**
Omar Sangha	**Sales Director**
John Bryce	**Production Director**

From their knowledge of the electronics business the company's founders believed there was a hole in the market for a high quality specialist range of semi-conductor test equipment. Using their combined expertise they were able to produce a convincing business plan. This enabled them from the outset to raise sufficient capital to launch DEL as a significant player in this particular sector.

Six years later the company has grown rapidly to a turnover of over £20 million, with net assets of over £3 million and with a workforce of over 200 employees. Details of DEL's accounts for the year to 31/3/02 are given in Appendix 1.

ACCOUNTING AND OTHER IT SYSTEMS

Most of the company's information systems have been in place for between 4-6 years and are in need of updating.

At present the principal systems are as follows:

- The main financial accounting system, including integrated general, purchase and sales ledgers. This operates in MSDOS and holds data in a non-relational database.

- A stand-alone full absorption costing system running on proprietary Wise software.

- A new integrated payroll and personnel database management system running in Windows 98, which was installed 3 months ago.

- A computer aided design/computer aided management (CAD/CAM) system, which is used for the design and control of the production of DEL products.

ACCOUNTING PERSONNEL

ELAINE CANDLER, BA, FCMA, FINANCE DIRECTOR

Elaine, aged 49, has overall responsibility for all accounting, finance, legal and IT issues. Elaine's primary responsibility is to manage the overall financial strategy of the business. Ensuring that capital investments are thoroughly appraised and in line with corporate strategy, that working capital levels are kept to a minimum, that the optimal mix of debt and equity funds DEL, and that its credit rating is maximized. In addition Elaine personally produces the annual company report, including its statutory accounts; deals with all banking and finance issues and fulfills the role of company secretary and handles all legal issues.

WILLIAM WHITELOW, AAT, COMPANY ACCOUNTANT

William, aged 59, has full day-by-day responsibility for the running of the DEL accounts department. He has been employed as company accountant since DEL was founded, and is AAT qualified. Originally William reported directly to the managing director, but since Elaine's appointment as finance director he has reported to her. William supervises the work of the accounting technicians and clerks running the transaction accounting systems i.e. the general ledger, purchase ledger, and sales ledger, together with the costing system and the payroll and personnel database management system. In addition, William personally produces the monthly management accounts, and approves all payments to suppliers.

The other five Accounts Department staff, which all report to William Whitelow, are:

SHARON EVANS, GENERAL LEDGER CLERK

Sharon, aged 26, is responsible for all data directly requiring input into the general ledger, and for producing the end of month trial balance. She is also responsible for maintaining the company's cashbook and its petty cash. Sharon has been in this job since she joined DEL three years ago, and has no accounting qualifications. Previously Sharon worked as a trainee personnel officer, but had to change job when her family moved area.

SUE MORAN, PURCHASE LEDGER CLERK

Sue, aged 36, is responsible for all data input into the purchase ledger, and for paying suppliers. Sue, who is William Whitelow's daughter, has been in this job for the past three years, and has foundation level AAT qualifications. Before working on the purchase ledger Sue spent the previous 8 months as the sales ledger clerk.

MOHAMED SINGH, SALES LEDGER CLERK AND CREDIT CONTROLLER

Mohamed, aged 27, is responsible for all data input into the sales ledger, and for the company's credit control. Mohamed has been in this job for the past three years since joining DEL, from Withern Electronics Ltd., where he was the purchase ledger clerk. Mohamed currently has no accounting or credit control qualifications, but has expressed an interest in acquiring some.

DAVID BROWNE, COSTING TECHNICIAN

David, aged 47, is responsible for costing DEL's products. He has been in this job since the company was formed, and his only other previous employer was a furniture manufacturer, where he worked after leaving school until the firm closed just over six years ago. His final position there was as credit controller. David has no accounting qualifications, and has on several occasions expressed his reluctance to undertake any form of personal development or training.

RACHEL FREY, PAYROLL & PERSONNEL DATABASE CLERK

Rachel, aged 22, is responsible for running the monthly payroll (for salaried staff) and weekly payroll (for hourly paid staff), and issuing P45's, P60's and so on. She is also responsible for maintaining the personnel database. Rachel was recruited to do this job two months ago, when the previous clerk left. Rachel has no accounting qualifications, and joined the company straight from university, where she obtained a pass degree in history. The software company who sold DEL the system gave Rachel three day's intensive training on the new payroll & personnel system.

The final member of the accounts team is you, **TONY BUSH, ACCOUNTING SYSTEMS TECHNICIAN.**

You report directly to Elaine Candler. You are aged 26, and are employed largely on reviewing accounting systems, plus any other project work that the finance director or company accountant may ask you to undertake. You have worked for DEL for the past two years and are hoping to complete your AAT qualifications this year. You have experience of working on both sales and general ledgers, but not at DEL.

BUSINESS & ACCOUNTING PRACTICES AND POLICIES

PURCHASES AND SUPPLIER PAYMENTS

The company buyer, George Stewart, is responsible for identifying and liaising with suppliers, and negotiating all contracts and prices with them. George has been in this position for the past four years.

The previous buyer had always followed a policy, set by the DEL board, of dealing with around 150 suppliers and playing one off against another in order to buy any materials or capital items at the lowest possible price available for that individual transaction. Three years ago, however, both George and William Whitelow had attended a seminar on "partnership sourcing", and had recommended to the board that a new policy of dealing with a much smaller number of suppliers on long-term contracts should be adopted. The board approved this change and DEL now operates with only around 30 regular suppliers, who are on two to three year contracts with annual price negotiations. The advantage of this policy to DEL is that it can get to know and understand 30 suppliers far better than it can 150, and can get the advantages of long-term stability in terms of product quality and prices.

Virtually all purchases are on 30-60 day credit terms. The purchase ledger clerk, Sue Moran, checks any new suppliers for financial stability.

All supplier invoices and goods received notes are sent initially to George Stewart, who is responsible for checking that the correct quantities have been received as ordered, and that the invoiced prices are correct. George then passes the approved invoices to Sue Moran who enters them into the purchase ledger, and at the same time makes the appropriate general ledger postings. Every month the purchase ledger system produces an aged creditors listing which identifies those suppliers now due for payment. The company accountant, William Whitelow, is responsible for approving the actual payments to be made, but bearing in mind the company's cash position at the time. Suppliers are, in fact, nearly always paid on time.

Finally, the computer system produces the actual cheques, which are then signed both by William Whitelow and by one of the four directors. Usually this will be Elaine Candler, but when she is away on business, which is quite often the case, Richard West generally countersigns them. Increasingly suppliers are paid by BACS, in which case the BACS payment authority is approved by William and then countersigned by one of the other directors. Neither the sales nor production directors are ever happy about countersigning all the individual cheques, because of the time involved, but are quite happy to put the one countersignature on the BACS payment authority form.

All company cheques are required to have two signatures, the authorised signatories being the four directors and the company accountant.

SALES AND CUSTOMER RECEIPTS

The company's sales force, led by Omar Sangha, are responsible for all dealings with existing customers and for identifying potential new ones. When a new customer is found, the company's policy is generally to trade with them on cash with an order basis of a three month trial period. The sales ledger clerk, Mohamed Singh, is responsible for credit checking these new customers, together with the relevant sales representative. This is to recommend a credit limit, which will apply after the three month trial period. All new credit limits and changes to existing limits are approved by the finance director, or in her absence by the managing director.

DEL has around 250 regular customers – 40 of whom account for 80% of the company's turnover.

The sales ledger clerk, Mohamed Singh, uses the goods dispatched listings as the trigger to produce sales invoices, which in accordance with Elaine Candler's instructions are sent out on a daily basis. All cheque payments received are sent to Mohamed who banks them also on a daily basis. Mohamed is responsible for all the postings to the sales ledger, and for the associated entries in the general ledger.

Sharon Evans produces a monthly bank reconciliation statement, which amongst other things reconciles the cashbook to the bank statement and the paying in book to the statement. The reconciliation is then checked by William Whitelow, who formally signs it off as being correct.

Mohamed produces a monthly aged debtors listing and all outstanding debtors more than one month overdue are reviewed with William Whitelow.

All outstanding debtors, more than three months overdue are reviewed both by Elaine Candler and by Omar Sangha.

PAYROLL AND PERSONNEL RECORDS

The company operates with two separate payrolls. Rachel Frey, the payroll & personnel database clerk runs the first every week to pay the hourly paid, largely the shop floor workers. Around 20% of these hourly paid employees are paid in cash, with the rest having payments made directly into their bank accounts via BACS. Those paid in cash collect their pay packets from Rachel's office every Friday, and those paid via BACS have their pay credited to their accounts on the same day. The second payroll is run three days before the last working day of each month to pay the monthly paid staff, which is either management, sales or office staff. All monthly paid employees are paid via BACS.

Once the two payrolls for the month have been finalised William Whitelow draws up manual cheques to the Inland Revenue in respect of income tax and NIC payments. William and one of the four directors sign these cheques.

As well as running the payroll, Rachel also maintains all the personnel records on the same integrated payroll and personnel database management system. This is DEL's newest system, having only been installed three months ago.

DIARY OF EVENTS WITHIN THE DEL ACCOUNTS
DEPARTMENT OVER THE PAST TWELVE MONTHS

March/April 2002

31/3/2002: This was the company's financial year end. These months were, therefore, characterised by the usual peak in workload for any accounts department at this time of the year. In several areas specific problems in meeting the year end closure routines were experienced.

Mohamed Singh faced considerable problems this month. In his capacity as credit controller (with a brief to reduce year end debts outstanding) he was fully occupied chasing up debtors during the month. This prevented him from keeping up with his work in his other role as sales ledger clerk. By the end of the month Mohamed had only completed the postings for a small amount of the transaction entries affecting the sales ledger, and was working over 60 hours a week (with paid overtime) to try and catch up. Only Sue Moran was sufficiently experienced in operating the sales ledger to be able to provide any meaningful help, but this was however, severely limited because as usual at the year end Sue had enough work of her own to get through. Also she was three years out of practice in working in this area.

Sharon Evans also had great difficulties in meeting the required year end deadlines. During the year Sharon is usually extremely busy during the week of the month-end period, but has relatively little to do during the rest of the month. She knows that the year end period in particular is going to stretch her to the limit, and always tries to get well ahead with her work on direct general ledger postings, the cash book and petty cash so that she can concentrate on producing the trial balance. Since, however, both the sales ledger and the purchase ledger were closed off later than scheduled Sharon, in turn, was unable to complete balancing the trial balance until nearly two weeks after the set date.

The payroll system (that is the system in use at this time, which was subsequently replaced in early January 2003) had been causing problems for quite some time. David Watts, who was the payroll clerk at this time, reported problems caused by its extreme slow running during the month. As well as 31/03 being the company's financial year end, the UK tax year ends on 05/04. This makes this an extremely busy time for the payroll clerk, since he was having to complete the normal payroll routines, he has also to ensure that the payroll closure ties in with DEL's internal year end timetable, and then produce the various forms and certificates required by the Inland revenue. Like Mohamed and Sharon, David was also behind schedule (in this case by four days) in terms of the DEL year end timetable.

These delays in finalising the transaction accounting meant that Elaine Candler, who always personally produces the statutory accounts, had to cancel or delay several important scheduled meetings with outside third parties in order to work full time on the statutory accounts. In particular, she and the managing director had to postpone a meeting with the company's bankers, which had been set to review the financial year 2001/2 accounts. This meeting was important because the company, in addition to renewing its annual overdraft facility was looking to raise a new £250,000 five year term loan to finance a replacement item of machinery.

The only element of light relief in the accounts department this month was a postcard from David Browne, costing technician, telling his colleagues that he was not really enjoying his annual skiing holiday because of the poor covering of snow this year. He did, however, report that the off piste activities were fine.

May 2002

In contrast to the traumas of the past two months, this was a fairly quiet and uneventful month.
Very little was seen of the finance director as she spent virtually the whole period off site, either with the company's auditors or in meetings with various banks.

William Whitelow largely concerned himself with reviewing outstanding supplier payments. As is normal practice at DEL, creditors are not generally paid the month before the full- year and half-year ends, but are then paid in the first two weeks of the following month. Since the company only operates with a relatively small number of suppliers, it is usually possible for Sue Moran, the purchase ledger clerk, to ring them and advise that their payments will be a few weeks late. Most suppliers accept that this tends to be standard business practice, and have no real problem with it. William, however, felt that a full review of the purchase ledger, and in particular of outstanding balances, would be a useful supervisory exercise.

As a result of the problems in failing to meet the year end calendar, Tony Bush was instructed by Elaine Candler to undertake a work rescheduling and training review. Firstly, Tony was asked to carry out a systematic review of the competencies of the five members of the accounts department (excluding William Whitelow), to recommend what their training needs are and to advise Elaine of the type of training that should be provided. Secondly, he was to recommend ways of rescheduling the work of the department in order to make the best possible use of both the people working in it and of the systems operated by it.

June 2002

Elaine Candler announced to the staff that the five year term loan for the new machinery had now finally been agreed, but with a different bank than the company's regular bankers.

A major problem mid-month was a power cut, due to fallen electricity cables, which lasted for nearly two days. Although the company does have a standby generator this is only sufficient to power the whole of the factory and offices for up to four hours.

The normal practice in the accounts department is to back up all systems at the close of business each day. However since, the power failure occurred in the late afternoon, this meant that all that day's work on all the ledgers, the costing system and the payroll was lost. During the following day the accounts staff could do very little other than basic manual clerical work, and when it became clear that the power would not be restored until late evening the managing director took the decision to close the entire factory and offices for the rest of the day on health and safety grounds.

By the month end the accounts department had managed to effectively catch up their lost work by working a large number of extra hours, as paid overtime. It was generally felt by the staff that their being individually absent for a day or so was never a real problem, except at the year-end and half year-ends. This is because there is usually sufficient slack in the system to allow for this. However, their being all effectively unable to work for two days did cause great difficulties because of the integrated nature of the transaction accounting system.

July 2002

Tony Bush reported back on the results of the work rescheduling and training review, and it was agreed that his recommendations would be implemented during the remainder of this financial year.

The old payroll system (that is in use at this time) has, as previously recorded been causing problems for quite some time. This month David Watts, the payroll clerk at this time, reported to Willam Whitelow that these regular problems of slow running and occasional crashes were continuing to get steadily worse as each month went by.

This system had been installed when the company and its accounts department were first set up, as a stand alone system running on spreadsheets on a PC. David Watts felt that, whilst this was alright for dealing with the 50 or so people employed at that time, it could no longer cope now that there were over 200 employees.

Since DEL does not have a personnel or HRM officer the personnel records are, by default, manually maintained by the payroll clerk. David and William both agreed that maintaining these manual personnel record cards for the steadily increasing number of employees was getting too overwhelming, and was causing David to duplicate work that he had already done for the payroll system.

August 2002

Tony Bush spent the first two weeks of this month sitting in with David Watts, with the two of them noting which problems occurred on the payroll system during which specific operations. At the end of this review both had reached the following conclusions. Firstly, that although the existing system could be updated and amended it would not make financial sense to do so, and it would be better to buy in a proprietary payroll software package. Secondly, it would make sense to acquire such a package that also integrated into it a personnel database that could to a large extent be maintained by the same entries as would need to be made for the payroll.

As usual, during August, there were problems caused by staff holidays. Although some aspects of the accounts department's work can be left for a couple of weeks, others, relating to the transaction accounting, always cause difficulties when they are not done on a day-by-day basis.

For example, no invoices were raised during the second and third weeks of the month because Mohamed Singh was on holiday.

September 2002

It was decided in principle by Elaine Candler that the company would invest in a new integrated payroll and personnel database software package.

William Whitelow, David Watts and Tony Bush are to form a steering group to produce a detailed specification of exactly what DEL requires. Then they need to look at the available packages that meet this specification and finally make a cost recommendation to the finance director. Since Tony and David had already started looking at suitable packages it was expected that the three would be able to make a recommendation within the next month or so.

October 2002

Three members of the accounts department staff undertook some form of training this month. These were Sharon Evans, Sue Moran and Mohamed Singh. Training had also been organised for David Browne, but unfortunately David missed it due to being away sick on the relevant three days.

November 2002

The steering committee for the new integrated payroll and personnel database duly reported back, and the selected package was ordered with a scheduled installation date from the software company of the first week in January 2003.

December 2002

Richard West, the managing director, has spent three days this week on a CIMA Master Course on fraud. At the end of the course and on returning to DEL, Richard had his PA make copies of extracts from part of the course material. This is a paper entitled " Fraud Risk Management – A Guide to Good Practice", and extracts from this are included as Appendix 2 to this case study.

January 2003

The new integrated payroll and personnel database was installed on time, and David Watts was due to begin a training programme on it when he announced that he was resigning, having found a better paid position elsewhere. A temp, familiar with the new system, was brought in to cover the payroll whilst a replacement for David was found. All work on maintaining the personnel records was put on hold. William Whitelow undertook to dual run the old system for the next two months' payroll runs as an added test of the new system.

February 2003

David Watts left the company this month, and Rachel Frey, a 22 year old history graduate from Central Polytechnic University, replaced him. The software company who provided DEL with the new payroll and personnel database package provided Rachel with an in-house three day intensive training course on the system.

Product costing was unable to be undertaken for two weeks due to the absence due to sickness of David Browne, the costing technician. Normally David is able to plan his work well in advance to cover his work before going away on holiday etc., but this unexpected sick leave obviously prevented him from doing this. Unfortunately no other member of staff had the detailed knowledge of the company's products to be able to stand in for David.

March 2003

There were various problems with the new payroll system, and Rachel Frey is getting very worried about coping with the end of tax year P60's, P11D's and so on. In particular, the changes to NIC contribution levels, announced by the Chancellor of the Exchequer in last year's autumn statement, will require immediate updates to this part of the system.

During the month Tony Bush interviewed all members of the accounts department in order to formally report back to the finance director on the update from the work rescheduling and training review.

Appendix 3 contains the notes of a conversation from the meeting between Tony Bush and Mohamed Singh held on 31/3/2003.

APPENDIX 1

Summarised Profit & Loss Account and Balance Sheet for Delmar Electronics Ltd. for year to 31/3/02

Profit & Loss account for year ended 31/3/02

	2002 £000	2001 £000
Sales	20,152	18,564
Operating profit	1,364	1,226
Exceptional gain	327	-
Net interest payable	(560)	(617)
Currency exchange gain/ (loss)	(415)	(306)
Profit on ordinary activities before tax	716	303
Taxation on profit on ordinary activities	(167)	(68)
Profit on ordinary activities after tax	549	235
Dividends	(183)	(78)
Profit retained for the year	366	157

Balance Sheet as at 31/3/03

	2002 £000	2001 £000
Fixed assets		
Intangible assets	312	264
Tangible assets	4,556	4,218
	4,868	4,482
Current assets		
Stocks	2,668	2,482
Debtors	5,846	4,127
Cash	361	103
	8,875	6,712
Creditors: amounts falling due within one year	(2,578)	(2,256)
Net current assets	6,297	4,456
Total assets less current liabilities	11,165	8,938
Creditors: amounts falling due after one year	(8,040)	(8,225)
Net assets	3,125	713

APPENDIX 2 - CHAPTER 2

RISK MANAGEMENT - AN OVERVIEW

Risks are the opportunities and dangers associated with uncertain future events. There is risk in any situation where there is a possibility of more than one outcome. The existence of risk leads in itself to uncertainty, but the level of uncertainty will vary both with knowledge and attitude. Risks may not even be recognised, but a lack of recognition does not alter their existence.

Risk management is the process of understanding the nature of such future events and, where they represent threats, making positive plans to counter them. This guide is primarily focused on managing the risk of fraud, but, first, this chapter looks at more general aspects of risk management. It is proposed that risk management will be covered in more depth in a future guide.

2.1 THE CONTEXT – CORPORATE GOVERNANCE

In recent years, the issue of corporate governance has been a major area for concern in many countries. In an early example, in the United States, the Treadway Commission 1987 report on fraudulent financial reporting confirmed the role and status of audit committees. Subsequently, the Securities and Exchange Commission (SEC) introduced the requirement that all SEC regulated companies should have an audit committee with a majority of non-executive directors. A subgroup of the Treadway Commission then developed a framework for internal control, providing detailed criteria for management to assess internal control systems and giving guidance for reporting publicly on internal control. In the UK, listed companies now have to meet the requirements of the Combined Code of Corporate Governance which calls, among other matters, for boards to establish systems of internal control and to review the effectiveness of these systems on a regular basis. Subsequently, the Turnbull Committee was set up to issue guidance to directors on how they should assess and report on their review of this effectiveness. The Committee made it clear that they considered that the establishment of embedded risk management practices key to effective internal control systems. While guidance is generally applicable to listed companies, the principles are relevant to all organisations. Fraud risk management practices are developing along the same lines.

Controls assurance

Controls assurance is the process whereby controls are reviewed by management and staff. There are various ways to conduct these exercises, from highly interactive workshops based on behavioural models at one end of the spectrum to pre-packaged self-audit internal control questionnaires at the other. These models all include monitoring and risk assessment among their principal components.

2.2 MANAGING RISK – THE RISK MANAGEMENT CYCLE

Risk management is an increasingly important process in many businesses and the process fits in well with the precepts of good corporate governance. The risk management cycle is an interactive process of identifying risks, assessing their impact, and prioritising actions to control and reduce risks.

Managing the risk of fraud is the same in principle as managing any other business risk. It is best approached systematically both at the organisational level e.g. by using ethics policies and anti-fraud policies, and at the operational level. A number of iterative steps should be taken:

1. Establish a risk management group and set goals.
2. Identify risk areas.
3. Understand and assess the scale of risk.
4. Develop a risk management strategy.
5. Implement the strategy and allocate responsibilities.
6. Implement and monitor implementation of the suggested controls.

Risk Management Cycle
pted from 'Managing the Risk of Fraud – A Guide for Managers', HM Treasury, 1997)

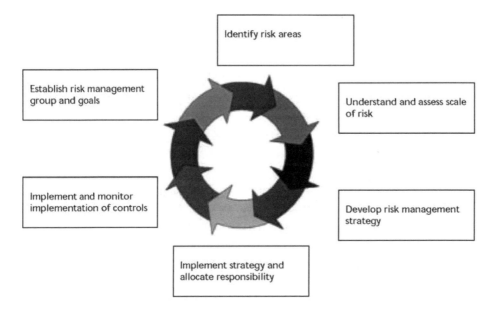

ESTABLISH A RISK MANAGEMENT GROUP AND SET GOALS

A risk management group should be established whose task it is to conduct reviews of the risks, which include the risk of fraud, faced by the business. The group will need to assess the risk appetite of the business (i.e. the level of risk the company is prepared to accept). It should then begin the process of understanding and assessing risk, prioritising, and developing a strategy to deal with the risks identified.

The risk management group should be responsible for reviewing systems and procedures, identifying and assessing the risks, and introducing the controls that are best suited to the business unit.

IDENTIFY RISK AREAS

Each risk in the overall risk model should be explored to identify how it potentially evolves through the organisation. It is important to ensure that the risk is carefully defined and explained to facilitate further analysis. The techniques of analysis include:

- workshops and interviews;
- brainstorming;
- questionnaires;
- process mapping;
- comparisons with other organisations;
- discussions with peers.

UNDERSTAND AND ASSESS THE SCALE OF RISK

Once risks have been identified, an assessment of possible impact and corresponding likelihood of occurrence should be made using consistent parameters that will enable the development of a prioritised risk analysis. In the planning stage management should agree on the most appropriate definition and number of categories to be used when assessing both likelihood and impact.

The assessment of the impact of the risk should not simply take account of the financial impact but should also consider the organisation's viability and reputation, and recognise the political and commercial sensitivities involved. The analysis should either be qualitative or quantitative, and should be consistent to allow comparisons. The qualitative approach usually involves grading risks in high, medium and low categories.

Impact

The assessment of the potential impact of a particular risk may be complicated by the fact that a range of possible outcomes may exist or that the risk may occur a number of times in a given period of time.

Such complications should be anticipated and a consistent approach adopted which, for example, may seek to estimate a worst case scenario over, say, a twelve-month time period.

Likelihood of occurrence

The likelihood of a risk occurring should be assessed on a gross, a net and a target basis.

The gross basis assesses the inherent likelihood of the event occurring in the absence of any processes which the organisation may have in place to reduce that likelihood.

The net basis assesses the likelihood, taking into account current conditions and processes to mitigate the chance of the event occurring.

The target likelihood of a risk occurring reflects the risk appetite of the organisation. Where the net likelihood and the target likelihood for a particular risk differ, this would indicate the need to alter the risk profile accordingly.

It is common practice to assess likelihood in terms of:

- high – probable;
- moderate – possible;
- low – remote.

An example of a risk analysis is contained in Appendix 7.

Analysing fraud risks

Fraud risk is one component of operational risk. Operational risk focuses on the risks associated with errors or events in transaction processing or other business operations. A fraud risk review considers whether these errors or events could be the result of a deliberate act designed to benefit the perpetrator. As a result, fraud risk reviews should be detailed exercises conducted by teams combining in-depth knowledge of the business and market with detailed knowledge and experience of fraud.

Risks such as those of false accounting or the theft of cash or assets needs to be considered for each part of the company's business. Frequently, businesses focus on a limited number of risks, most commonly on third-party thefts. To avoid this, the risks should be classified by reference to the possible type of offence and the potential perpetrator(s). The following matrix developed by Ernst and Young ('the Ernst and Young model') can be used:

Department/ area	Details of risk area	Management	Employees	Third parties	Collusion
False accounting					
Theft					

These will need to be assessed for each area and process of the business, for example, cash payments, cash receipts, sales, purchasing, expenses, inventory, payroll, fixed assets, loans, etc.

DEVELOP A RISK MANAGEMENT STRATEGY

Once the risks have been identified and assessed, and the organisation's risk appetite has been set, strategies can be developed by the risk management group to deal with each risk that has been identified. Strategies could include:

- ignoring small risks (but ensuring that they remain under cyclical review);
- contractual transfer of risk;
- risk avoidance;
- risk reduction via controls and procedures;
- transferring risks to insurers.

2.7 IMPLEMENT THE STRATEGY AND ALLOCATE RESPONSIBILITIES

The chosen strategy should be allocated and communicated to those responsible for implementation. For the plan to be effective it is essential that responsibility for each specific action is assigned to the appropriate operational manager and, that clear target dates are established for each action for the plan to be effective. It is also important to obtain the co-operation of those responsible for the strategy, by the use of means such as formal communication, seminars, action plans and adjustments to budgets.

2.8 IMPLEMENT AND MONITOR IMPLEMENTATION OF THE SUGGESTED CONTROLS

The chosen strategy may require the implementation of new controls or the modification of existing controls. Businesses are dynamic and the controls that are in place will need to be monitored to assess whether or not they are succeeding in their objectives. The risk management group should also be empowered to monitor the effectiveness of the actions being taken in each specific area as these can be affected by internal and external factors, such as changes in the marketplace or the introduction of new computer systems.

Summary

- There are risks in most situations. Risk management is an important element of corporate governance and every organisation should review their risk status and develop their approach as described in the Risk Management Cycle in 2.2 above.

The following chapters will expand on some aspects of this process.

CHAPTER 5

RESPONDING TO FRAUD

An organisation's approach to fraud should be described in its fraud policy and fraud response plan. A sample policy and example plan are contained in Appendices 1 and 2 respectively. This chapter expands on parts of the outline plan where they have not already been covered in earlier chapters and highlights some issues and considerations. Paragraph headings in this chapter are those which should form the basis of the fraud response plan and relate to the actions in the outline response plan in Appendix 2.

5.1 THE PURPOSE OF THE FRAUD RESPONSE PLAN

The fraud response plan is a formal means of setting down clearly the arrangements which are in place for dealing with suspected cases of theft, fraud or corruption. It is intended to provide procedures which allow for evidence gathering and collation in a manner which will facilitate informed decision-making, while ensuring that evidence gathered will be admissible in the event of any civil or criminal action. Other benefits arising from the publication of a corporate fraud response plan are its deterrence value and the likelihood that it will reduce the tendency to panic. It can help restrict damage and minimise losses, enable the organisation to retain market confidence, and help to ensure the integrity of evidence.

5.2 CORPORATE POLICY

The fraud response plan should reiterate the organisation's commitment to high legal, ethical and moral standards in all its activities and its approach to dealing with those who fail to meet those standards. It is important that all those working in the organisation are aware of the risk of fraud and other illegal acts such as dishonesty or damage to property. As discussed in Chapter 3, they should be clear about the means of enforcing the rules or controls which the organisation has in place to counter such risks and be aware of how to report any suspicions they may have. The fraud response plan is the means by which this information is relayed to all members of staff and, possibly, other stakeholders, such as customers, suppliers, and shareholders.

5.3 FRAUDULENT ACTIVITIES

As has been explained in Chapter 1, there is no universal legal definition of 'fraud' as an offence but the term encompasses criminal offences involving the obtaining of some benefit, or causing detriment of some person or organisation by dishonest means. This section could provide for legal definitions or simply a list of activities which would or could be considered fraudulent.

5.4 ROLES AND RESPONSIBILITIES

The division of responsibilities for fraud management will vary from one organisation to the next, depending on the size, industry, culture and other factors. However, the following are some general guidelines which can be adapted to suit the individual circumstances.

Managers and supervisors

Generally managers and supervisors are in a position to take responsibility for detecting fraud, misappropriation, and other irregularities in their area. Staff must assist management by reporting any suspected irregularities. Managers, and supervisors, should be provided with a response card, or aide-memoire, detailing how they should respond to a reported incidence of fraud. The aide-memoire should include a list of contacts with telephone numbers.

Director of finance

The director of finance will often have overall responsibility for the organisation's response to fraud, including the responsibility for co-ordinating any investigation and for keeping the fraud response plan up to date. He will hold the master copy of the fraud response plan, and should have his own aide-memoire to assist with the management of the investigation. He will also be responsible for maintaining the 'investigation log'.

Fraud officer

In large organisations it may be necessary designate a senior manager as the fraud officer in place of the finance director, with responsibility for initiating and overseeing all fraud investigations, for implementing the fraud response plan and for any follow-up actions. The fraud officer should be authorised to receive inquiries from staff confidentially and anonymously, and be given the authority to act and/or provide advice according to individual circumstances, and without recourse to senior management for approval. He will manage any internal investigations and act as a liaison officer with all other interested parties both internal, and external, including police, regulators and auditors. The fraud officer should have his own job description, appropriate to the role, an extended list of contacts and his own response card. One of his primary tasks would be the updating of the 'investigation log'.

In the event that the fraud officer's superior is a suspect, he should report to a more senior manager or non-executive director, perhaps the chair of the audit committee.

Human resources

The human resources department will usually have responsibility for any internal disciplinary procedures, which must be in line with, and support, the fraud policy statement and fraud response plan. Their advice should be sought in relation to the organisation's personnel management strategies, individual employment histories, and issues relating to employment law, or equal opportunities.

Audit committee (where applicable)

The audit committee should take responsibility for reviewing the organisation's performance in fraud prevention, reviewing the log of cases at least once a year and reporting any significant matters to the board. If a suspicion involves the nominated fraud contact or an executive director the matter should be reported directly to the chairman of the audit committee. In small companies a nominated non-executive director may fulfil the role of the audit committee.

Internal auditors (where applicable)

Where an organisation has its own internal audit department the likelihood is that the task of investigating any incidence of fraud would fall to them. It may be appropriate to designate specific auditors as 'fraud' specialists and to ensure that they have the appropriate skills and knowledge to undertake the task.

External auditors (where applicable)

An organisation without its own internal audit department may consider consulting their external auditors should they discover a 'fraud', if only to obtain the expertise to establish the level of loss. However, they may also be in a position to provide expert assistance from elsewhere within the firm; such as from a specialist fraud investigation group. A decision to call on external auditors should, however, be considered carefully as there is always the possibility that if the auditor has missed obvious fraud alerts, the organisation may eventually seek damages from its auditor.

Legal advisors (internal or external)

Legal advice should be sought immediately a 'fraud' is reported, irrespective of the route it is intended to follow. Specific advice would include such issues as guidance on civil, internal and criminal responses, and recovery of assets.

IS/IT staff

IS/IT staff can provide technical advice on IT security, capability and access. If computers have been utilised to commit the fraud, or if they are required for evidential purposes specialist advice must be sought immediately.

Public relations

Organisations with a high profile, e.g. larger businesses, public sector or charities, may wish to consider briefing their PR staff so they can prepare a brief for the press in the event that news of a fraud becomes public.

Police

When the police are consulted, if at all, is a matter of internal policy. However, if it is policy to prosecute all those suspected of fraud then the police should be involved at the outset of any investigation as any unnecessary delay could diminish the likelihood of success. In respect of public bodies, Audit Commission guidance states that the police/ external auditors should be informed immediately fraud is suspected.

External consultants

Any organisation could consider bringing in specialist investigation skills from outside the organisation. Many such specialist firms exist to provide a discreet investigation and/or asset recovery service in accordance with their clients' instructions.

Insurers

The timeframe for a report to fidelity insurers, and any additional requirements should be laid down in the insurance document.

ORGANISATION'S OBJECTIVES WITH RESPECT TO FRAUD

The organisation's policy may include any or all of the following preferred outcomes in dealing with fraud.

Internal disciplinary action

In accordance with the organisations personnel and disciplinary guidelines.

A civil response

This is the subject of a separate supplement to this guide which will be published shortly.

Criminal prosecution

Whereby action is taken against the individual(s) concerned in a police managed enquiry.

A parallel response

Where civil action to recover misappropriated assets is taken in parallel with a police investigation.

5.6 THE RESPONSE

Reporting suspicions

The procedures for reporting fraud should be spelt out clearly and succinctly. This may be by means of a formal whistleblowing policy but the procedures should also be summarised within the fraud response plan.

Establish an investigation team

After recording details of the allegations the finance director, or the fraud officer, as appropriate, should call together the investigation team plus their advisors. This could involve any, or all, of those listed above with the possible exception of insurers.

Formulate a response

The objectives of the investigation should be clearly identified, as should the resources required, the scope of the investigation, and the timescale. The investigating team's objectives will be driven by the organisations attitude to fraud; that is internal action, civil response, prosecution of offenders, or some form of parallel response. An action plan should be prepared and roles and responsibilities should be delegated in accordance with the skills and experience of the individuals involved. The individual in overall control of the investigation should be clearly identified as should the powers available to team members. Reporting procedures and evidence handling and recording procedures should be clearly understood by all concerned.

5.7 THE INVESTIGATION

Preservation of evidence

A key consideration in any investigation must always be how to secure or preserve sufficient evidence to prove fraud. If a criminal act is suspected, the police should be consulted at once before any overt action is taken, otherwise suspects may be alerted and evidence removed or destroyed.

In English and Welsh law, for the purposes of criminal proceedings, the admissibility of evidence is governed by the Police and Criminal Evidence Act (PACE). In addition, the Criminal Procedures and Investigations Act 1996 provides a statutory framework and code of practice for disclosure of material collected during the course of investigations. Although PACE does not apply in civil or disciplinary proceedings it should nevertheless be regarded as best practice. If an individual does end up being charged with a criminal offence (and this may not be planned at the outset of the investigation), all investigations and relevant evidence will be open to discovery by that individual's defence. It is, therefore, important that proper records are kept from the outset, including accurate notes of when, where and from whom the evidence was obtained and by whom. The police, or legal advisors, will be able to advise on how this should be done.

Physical evidence

It is vitally important that control is taken of any physical evidence before the opportunity arises for it to be removed or destroyed by the suspect(s). Physical evidence may therefore need to be seized at an early stage in the investigation, before any witness statements are collected or interviews conducted. If appropriate, written consent should be obtained from the department or branch manager before any items are removed. This can be done with senior management authority as the items are the organisation's own property. Similarly, electronic evidence must be secured before it can be tampered with.

If an internal investigation is being conducted then clearly an organisation has a right to access its own records and may bring disciplinary action against any member of staff who tries to prevent this. Where physical evidence is owned or held by other organisations or individuals who are not employees it may be necessary to obtain a court order or injunction to secure access to or to allow seizure of the evidence. The exact means of obtaining physical evidence depends on the particular circumstances of the case and whether criminal or civil action is being pursued, or both.

When taking control of any physical evidence, original material is essential – photocopies are not acceptable. Records should be kept of the time that it was taken and the place that it was taken from. If evidence consists of several items, for example many documents, each one should be tagged with a reference number, which corresponds with the written record. Taking photographs or video recordings of the scene may also prove helpful.

When conducting investigations it is essential to be mindful of the provisions of the Human Rights Act, in particular the rights to privacy and to a fair trial or hearing.

Interviews (general)

Managers are quite entitled to interview staff under their direction and to ask them to account for assets which were, or are, under their direct control, or to explain their performance in respect of the management or supervision of specific employees. However, the point at which it is considered that there are reasonable grounds for suspicion of an individual is the point where questioning should be stopped and the individual advised that their actions will be the subject of a formal investigation (should criminal prosecution be considered). From this moment on any interviews should be conducted by trained personnel, or by police officers. Detailed notes should be kept of questions and answers, and interviews should be taped if possible.

Statements from witnesses

If a witness is prepared to give a written statement, it is good practice for someone else, normally a trained, or experienced manager, to take a chronological record of events using the witness's own words. The witness must be happy to sign the resulting document as a true record. The involvement of an independent person usually helps to confine the statements to the relevant facts and the witness should also be given the opportunity to be supported by a 'friend' or trade union official.

Statements from suspects

If a criminal act is suspected the requirements of PACE, and other legislation, must be considered before any interview with a suspect takes place since compliance determines whether evidence is admissible in criminal proceedings. In any interview under caution the interviewer must ensure that they fully understand the requirements of PACE, as laid down in the codes of practice issued in accordance with S66 of the Act, before initiating the interview. As PACE is essentially a matter for police officers and other trained investigators, if the need for an interview under caution arises, police involvement should again be considered. Section 67 of the Act states – 'Persons other than police officers who are charged with the duty of investigating offences, shall ...... have regard to any relevant provision of the code.' Failure to observe the codes of practice may therefore jeopardise vital evidence, rendering it useless.

In practice, therefore, it is suggested that interviews should only be conducted by trained personnel with advice and guidance from the organisations legal advisors, or the police. This guidance could be supported by means of a 'brief' or an aide-memoire for the personnel concerned and supplemented with formal training.

5.8 FOLLOW-UP ACTION

Lessons learned

There are lessons to be learned from every identified incident of fraud, and the organisation's willingness to learn from experience is as important as any other response. The larger organisation may consider establishing a special group to examine the circumstances and conditions which allowed the fraud to occur with a view to making a report to senior management detailing improvements to systems and procedures. A smaller organisation may consider discussing the issues with some of its more experienced people with the same objectives in mind.

Management response

Internal reviews

Having had one incident of fraud, the organisation may consider a fundamental review of all of its system and procedures so as to identify any other potential system failures. Changes to the policy or systems should be implemented as soon as possible.

Implement changes

Should weaknesses have been identified it can only be of benefit to the organisation to take the appropriate remedial action. Recent statistics have confirmed once again that many organisations suffer more than one incident of fraud per annum.

Annual report

An annual report should be submitted to the board of all investigations carried out, outcomes and lessor learned.

APPENDIX 3

Notes of a conversation from the meeting between Tony Bush and Mohamed Singh held on 31/3/2003.

Tony: Hello Mohamed. As you know I'm interviewing all staff in order to monitor how the changes are going from the work rescheduling and training review.

Mohamed: Erm… right…ok.

Tony: So how IS it going?

Mohamed: Tony, I've been wanting to talk with you anyway because I erm… I think we've got a major problem with the way that the purchasing system is being operated.

Tony: William is your line manager. Have you talked to him about this?

Mohamed: Erm well yes I would have done – but the thing is I think that whatever is going on he's well sort of involved in it. I'm also a bit nervous about bringing this up with Elaine – I don't want to make a complete fool of myself if I'm wrong. In any event, as you know, she's in hospital recovering from surgery this week..

Tony: This sounds rather serious, Mohamed. What do you mean?

Mohamed: You'll remember, of course, that a few months ago you were asked to advise on a work rescheduling and training review, and that – as part of this – Sue Moran and myself were trained to cover each others work…

Tony: Of course I remember….

Mohamed: Well the thing is whenever I do swap with or cover for Sue, and I've done this perhaps twenty times now, I've never seen any invoices or purchase orders or dealt with any paperwork at all for one of our suppliers – a company called Raymond Briggs Ltd. We've only got around 30 creditors and so it seems odd that this one never comes through on my days on the purchase ledger.

Tony: Go on....

Mohamed: Erm well...I've looked into the company's records on the purchase ledger, and it seems that we've dealt with them for the past 3 years, but apart from this there's very little information on the system. Far less than for most of our suppliers in fact.

 I then went to see George Stewart about Briggs Ltd. and he immediately clammed up. The next morning I saw him in William Whitelow's office – which is also odd because in all the time I've worked here I can't recall seeing George in the accounts department at all.

Tony: Has this supplier ever been paid whilst you've been working on the purchase ledger?

Mohamed: I thought you might ask me that! The answer is no. I've checked back and every payment has been made while Sue Moran has been working on the purchase ledger.

Tony: Leave this with me – I'll get back to you on it later today.

CANDIDATE'S BRIEFING FOR A PROJECT REPORT BASED UPON THIS CASE STUDY.

Candidates who do not have the opportunity to undertake some form of work-based project are able to provide evidence of competence in this unit by writing a similar project report, but based on the material in this case study. The total length of the report should not exceed 4,000 words.

Specifically candidates should write a report, which demonstrates their underpinning knowledge and understanding of:

The Business environment

- External regulations affecting accounting practices (10.2)
- Common types of fraud (10.2)
- The implications of fraud (10.2)

Management techniques

- Methods of work planning and scheduling (10.1)
- Personal time management techniques (10.1)
- Methods of measuring cost-effectiveness (10.2)
- Methods of fraud detection within accounting systems (10.2)
- Techniques for influencing and negotiating with decision makers & resource holders (10.2)

Management principles and theory

- Principles of supervision and delegation (10.1)
- Principles of creating effective inter-personal relationships, team building and staff motivation (10.1)

The organisation

- The impact on an accounting system of organisational structure, Management Information Systems, administrative systems and procedures and the nature of its business transactions (10.1, 10.2)

- The organisation's business and its relationships with external stakeholders (10.1,10.2)
- The purpose, structure and organisation of the accounting system and its inter-relation with other internal functions (10.2)
- The control of resources by individuals within the organisation (10.1)

This can be demonstrated by writing a project report of up to 4,000 words, addressed to Elaine Candler - the finance director, which covers the following:

- **The co-ordination of work activities within DEL's accounting environment**

The candidate must demonstrate his/her ability to plan and co-ordinate DEL's accounts department's work activities effectively. Including setting and monitoring realistic objectives, targets and deadlines and managing people so that these can be met. In addition the candidate needs to show that he/she can develop contingency plans to deal with a range of problems that may detract from the organisation meeting these objectives, targets and deadlines.

- **Identification of opportunities to improve the effectiveness of DEL's accounting system**

The Candidate must demonstrate his/her ability to identify weaknesses in DEL's accounting system, and making recommendations to rectify these; to consider the impact that these would have on the organisation; to update the system to comply for example with legislative changes; and to subsequently check that the post-change output is now correct.

The project report should be both holistic and strategic in nature. That is, the candidate should report on each of the detailed areas listed below, and then bring these together in an integrated way so that the overall position can be seen. From this he/she should then identify perhaps 4-6 major issues, which are of strategic importance to DEL.

In detail the project should include:

- How the candidate would plan and monitor work routines to meet DEL's organisational time schedules and to make the best use of both their human and physical resources (PC A). Planning and scheduling this project report for completion to standard and on time will also provide evidence towards PC A.

- The systematic review of staff competencies and training needs, together with details of the training actually arranged (PC B).

- Contingency planning for possible emergencies, (e.g. computer system not being fully functional, staff absences, and changes in work patterns and demands) (PC C).

- How the candidate would communicate work methods and schedules to colleagues so that they have understood what is expected of them (PC D).

- How the candidate would monitor work activities closely against quality standards to ensure they are being met (PC E).

- How the candidate would co-ordinate work activities effectively against work plans and contingency plans (PC F).

- How the candidate would encourage colleagues to report promptly, issues beyond their authority and expertise. How he/she would resolve these where possible (PC G), or otherwise refer such issues to the appropriate person to resolve them (PC H).

- A situation analysis of the accounting system under scrutiny (e.g. a SWOT analysis), which will generate evidence towards performance criteria PCs A & B.

- Evidence of resulting recommendations made to the appropriate people in a clear understandable format and supported by a clear rationale. This will generate evidence towards PCs D & E. All assumptions made should be clearly listed.

- Evidence of research, pointing towards potential areas of fraud within DEL's accounting system (e.g. teeming and lading, fictitious employees or suppliers). Research into appropriate fraud risk standards, including the extracts provided in the case study, will generate evidence for PC B. Candidates are advised to use some form of matrix approach towards grading the various elements of risk.

- How the candidate would undertake a regular review of methods of operating, providing evidence for PC C.

- How the candidate would update the system in accordance with both internal factors (e.g. changes in the organisational structure, responses to customer surveys) and external factors (e.g. changes in company law, VAT rates, FRS's) that require such updates to be made. This provides evidence for PC F - SWOT and PEST analyses respectively would be useful here.

Any of the above evidence that does not sit naturally within the project report should be included as additional evidence in the appendices to it. If the listed Performance Criteria and Underpinning Knowledge and Understanding have NOT been addressed sufficiently by the project content documented, then assessor questioning MUST be employed to address any gaps.

ALL Performance Criteria and Underpinning Knowledge and Understanding must be evidenced.

AAT SAMPLE SIMULATION
UNIT 10

MANAGING SYSTEMS AND PEOPLE IN THE ACCOUNTING ENVIRONMENT

ANSWERS

SUGGESTED APPROACH

Before producing our suggested report based on the Delmar Electronics Ltd Case Study in this section we will consider how to go about producing the report and the general approach you should take to such a large case study and 4,000 word report.

Initial read through

You are given a lot of information about Delmar Electronics Ltd - background information, accounting personnel details and business and accounting practices and policies. As a starting point read fairly quickly through all of the information given so that you are aware of the overall content of the case study.

Candidate's briefing notes

Next read through the candidate's briefing notes for the project report in detail as this is telling you precisely what you need to do. Note that the report is to be addressed to Elaine Candler, the financial director and that it is to cover the following main topics:

- planning and coordinating the accounts department's work activities

- setting and monitoring targets and deadlines

- managing people so that these targets and deadlines can be met

- develop contingency plans

- identify weaknesses in the accounting system (using a SWOT analysis)

- make recommendations to rectify these weaknesses and consider the impact of these on the organisation

- update the system to comply with changes and check that the post change output is correct.

This should give you some idea of the types of topics that you will need cover in your report.

You are also given guidance on how to approach the content of your report. You are told that the report should be both 'holistic' and 'strategic'. This means that you should approach each issue separately initially and then bring them all together to form a conclusion as to what the major issues of strategic importance are to DEL.

Detailed read through

At this point return to the case study itself and read it through, this time in detail. You may find it useful to make various notes or draft diagrams as you read through. For example the following might be useful as you progress through your report:

- note the size of the company both in terms of turnover and net assets and number of employees

- details of the computer systems the company has

- an organisation chart for the accounts department noting the roles of each individual

- note that you are Tony Bush in this case study, the accounting systems technician

- details of how the purchases and supplier payments system works

- details of how the sales and receipts system works

- details of how the payroll system works

You then move on to the diary of events over the last year - again make notes / highlight facts that might appear important given the Performance Criteria that should be covered by this report. Your notes might include the following:

- the year end work scheduling problems

- possible contingency plan for loss of the computer system again as in the power cut

- staff holiday problems in August

- the reluctance of David Browne to attend any training courses

- fraud aspects highlighted by the managing director

- the problems caused by David Browne's two weeks of sick leave

- Rachel Frey's problems with her workload

Appendix 1

In appendix 1 you are given the financial statements of DEL Ltd for the year ending 31 March 2002. Although there is little detail given you can ascertain that there has been little change in operating profit margin from 2001 to 2002 but that the most significant factor on the balance sheet at 31 March 2002 was a 42% increase in year end debtors.

student notes✍

Appendix 2

Appendix 2 is a number of chapters from a paper on Risk Management. A of the relevant knowledge is included in Chapter 7 so just quickly rea through the appendix and refer back to Chapter 7 if you feel that you nee to.

Appendix 3

Appendix 3 gives you the transcript of a conversation during an apprais meeting between Tony Bush and Mohammed Singh. Clearly Mohammed ha some concerns about a potential fraud in the purchases system and you mu consider carefully how you would deal with this in your report.

Planning your report

With detailed knowledge of the case study content and what is required your report, you can start to plan the contents of the main body of yo report. Consider all of the areas that will be covered by your report, no them down and put them into a logical order.

You are writing this report from the perspective of Tony Bush, the accountir systems technician, in terms of what he has done over the past year and wh he believes should be done in the future. Therefore the areas that you w probably cover are:

- staff competencies and training needs analysis
- rescheduling of work
- contingency planning
- SWOT analysis of the accounting system
- consideration of potential areas of fraud
- recommendations for changes
- updates to the system

Form of your report

At this stage before you start the detailed writing of your report it is probably worthwhile to look back to Chapter 8 on writing your report in order to remind yourself of the overall presentation of a report. There are a number of sections to a report, some of which can be approached from the start but others that cannot be completed until the end of your work:

Title: The report will be covering a number of topics so keep the title fairly general.

Contents: This will need to be done when you have finished.

Summary: Again this cannot be done until the rest of the report is finished.

Terms of reference: This is probably a good place to start in order to get all of your thoughts clear about how the report is to work.

Methodology: This is best to do as you go along. If you do collect or analyse data, or consult documents then note them down as you do it. This section will probably not be relevant for this type of report.

Body of the report: The hard work element!

Conclusions: These cannot be reached until you have finished each of the individual sections of the report but they are a very important element of the report and therefore ensure that you leave enough time to complete this section.

Recommendations: As with the conclusion this is extremely important to your report and covers a number of performance criteria. You cannot decide upon any recommendations until you have completed the main body of the report so ensure that you leave enough time for this section.

Appendices: If you do carry out any calculations or analyses which are not to appear in the main body of the report include them here and reference the main body of the report to them.

Time to start!

SUGGESTED REPORT

REPORT

To: Elaine Candler, Finance Director

From: Tony Bush
Accounting Systems Technician

Date: April 2003

Subject: Review of DEL Ltd accounting function and systems

Contents

Staff competencies and training needs review
Rescheduling of work activities
Contingency planning
Review of the accounting system
Consideration of potential areas of fraud
Reporting of issues by colleagues

Summary

This report assesses the coordination of work activities within the accountir function of DEL Ltd by considering the competencies of the accountir function's staff and any training needs they may have. Following on from th the rescheduling and coordination of the accounting function's work considered including the possibility of contingency plans for computer failu and staff absences. The report also identifies opportunities to improve th effectiveness of DEL's accounting system by assessing the current accountir system and considering potential areas of fraud within the system.

Terms of reference

This report has been written to the finance director, Elaine Candler, in ord to assess the coordination of work activities within the accounting function DEL Ltd and to identify opportunities to improve the effectiveness of DE accounting system. The report will consider the training and work scheduli activities that have taken place in the last year, together with th consideration of contingency plans which are considered necessary bas upon the experiences of the accounting function. The report also assesses th current accounting system for strengths and weaknesses in order to ma recommendations for potential improvements. The report concludes with th major issues of strategic importance to the DEL Ltd accounting function.

·aff competencies and training needs review

¬ring the year to 31 March 2003 there have been a number of problems ¬th staffing and meeting of deadlines at key times. This requires some ¬cheduling of work (see next section) and an attempt to ensure that the staff ¬thin the accounting function become multi- skilled so that in times of staff ¬rtages or tight deadlines each member of staff can perform more than one ¬ction. In order to do this the existing competencies of the staff of the ¬ounting function were analysed to determine what, if any, training was ¬eded for each member of staff.

¬e organisation chart, current duties, accounting qualifications and ¬perience of each member of the accounting function are set out in ¬pendix 1 to this report. The full assessment of each member of the ¬ounting function staff is now given:

¬aron Evans, General ledger clerk

¬aron's duties at the end of each month include the preparation of the ¬nth end trial balance and bank reconciliation and therefore the last week ¬ each is month is always busy for her. However for the remainder of the ¬nth Sharon is not stretched as her duties are to maintain the cash book ¬d petty cash book and to make the general ledger entries.

¬aron has no accounting qualifications but having been with DEL Ltd for the ¬ three years is experienced within her role. Her background is that of a ¬sonnel officer and therefore, in order to increase her workload, and to ¬uce that of Rachel Frey, Sharon could become involved in the ¬intenance of the personnel database but will require training for the new ¬em.

¬ Moran, Purchase ledger clerk

¬ concentrates on the purchase ledger but has previous experience as the ¬s ledger clerk. She should receive training from Mohammed Singh on the ¬s ledger work in order to be competent to carry out sales ledger functions ¬ a regular basis and also at times when additional help is required.

¬ has her foundation level AAT qualification and should be encouraged to ¬tinue with her studies. In order to support her further studies and also to ¬vide an additional employee who can deal with the costing of the ¬npany's products, Sue should be trained by David Browne in the costing ¬ects of the accounting function.

¬hammed Singh, sales ledger clerk and credit controller

¬hammed is responsible for not only all sales ledger input but also for credit ¬trol and the chasing of bad debts. His past experience has been within ¬ purchase ledger section of another company and therefore he could use

269

that experience to be trained by Sue Moran in the workings of DE
purchase ledger in order to be able to work in this area when required.

Mohammed has no accounting qualifications but has expressed interest
acquiring some and therefore should be encouraged to study, proba
initially for the AAT Foundation level.

David Browne

David is solely responsible for costing the company's products and no oth
person in the department has the knowledge to carry out these functio
David himself has past experience of credit control and as such could rece
on the job training from Mohammed in order to help out with credit cont
particularly around the year end.

David appears to have no career or personal development plan and inde
missed his planned training in October 2002.

Rachel Frey payroll and personnel database clerk

Rachel is new to the job having only joined the company in February 20
She has received only three days of internal training to use the new compu
system and is currently struggling to carry out all of her tasks. Rachel sho
be provided with help to deal with the new system and also additio
software training. As a new employee, Rachel's career and perso
development should be considered and discussed with her.

Rescheduling of work activities

Significant problems have been found within the accounting function at
year end, at times of staff sickness and during popular holiday periods s
as August. These problems have resulted in significant delays both in reg
transactions and accounting and also in the preparation of the anr
financial statements.

Current problems with work activities

These problems appear to have been caused by two main factors. Fir
prior to the competencies and training needs review, each of the member
the accounting function was only able to carry out their own particular j
so at times of sickness or holiday there is no one else in the departmen
carry out the missing employee's tasks. The second problem seems to be
at the month end and year end in particular some members of the team s
as Sharon Evans are overloaded with tasks whereas other such as Da
Browne are not really affected by the month or year end routine.

Possible solutions to these problems

One method of dealing with these problem times of the year is to ensure
the staff within the accounting function are multi-skilled, with each mem
of the team not only being able to carry out their general duties but be
trained and capable of carrying out at least one other function within

counts department. However training is not enough and the staff must be scheduled to carry out their new functions regularly otherwise the training will soon be forgotten. The use of multi-skilled staff regularly carrying out their colleagues' main duties can also help to guard against the possibility of fraudulent activities.

On its own the multi-skilling of staff will not solve the staffing problem at the critical month and year ends. Therefore an assessment of the entire department's tasks is required in order to determine which tasks are specifically required at these times such as monthly payroll, monthly reconciliations, closing ledger accounts and preparing a trial balance. The other tasks of the department will be those that can be carried out at less busy periods such as chasing bad debts, costing and updating of personnel records.

The work of the staff in the department should be rescheduled to ensure that each staff using their new skills all of the month and year end tasks can be carried out on time, whilst the general work can be completed at less busy times of the year. This means that staff will be working towards a departmental timetable rather than simply according to their own individual function.

contingency planning

During the past year there have been examples of major problems within the accounting function for which the company as yet has no plans. In June 2002, due to power failure, all members of the accounting function were effectively unable to work for two days and had to work large amounts of paid overtime in order to catch up for the lost work. In August 2002 there were problems due to staff absences on holiday which resulted in no invoices being raised for two weeks which obviously has a significant effect on the company's cash flow.

Therefore it would appear to be necessary to consider contingency plans for both computer failure and staff absences in order to be better prepared in future.

What is a contingency plan?

A contingency is an event or risk that may or may not happen. Contingency plans are plans of how to deal with risks that are recognised but by their very nature are unlikely, although possible. Contingency planning will involve assessing unplanned events which may occur from time to time. The assessment will involve determining:

- the probability of the event happening
- the level of impact of the event on the business

Where there is a reasonable probability of the event happening and the effect on business would be material, a contingency plan should normally be

student notes✐

considered. Whether or not a contingency plan is put in place will depe[...]
upon a cost-benefit analysis of each contingency.

Computer failure

As far as the accounting function is concerned the computer system consi[...]
of three stand alone elements:

- the main financial accounting system, with integrated gener[...]
  purchase and sales ledgers

- the costing system

- the payroll and personnel database management system

In general terms the most important method of dealing with any compu[...]
failure is regular backup of data. This currently happens daily, at the end[...]
each day, which appears reasonable, as in the worst case scenario only c[...]
day of input will be lost. However other ways of dealing with compu[...]
failure should be considered and a cost-benefit analysis carried out.

If there is a failure of either the costing system or the payroll and person[...]
system, on the whole this will mean the loss of at maximum one day of w[...]
which in the normal course of business can be caught up by David Brow[...]
or Rachel Frey. The exception to this might be a computer failure at either [...]
end of a week, for the weekly payroll, or the end of the month, for [...]
monthly payroll. Consideration should be given to a subscription to[...]
computer bureau service which would enable the payroll to be run on [...]
bureau's system if there were failure of DEL's payroll system at a critical tir[...]

The failure of the main financial accounting system is likely to have a m[...]
significant effect and an attempt to determine the cost of such a fail[...]
should be made. When the system failed due to a power cut in June 2([...]
the cost was significant paid overtime. This might be compared to the c[...]
of subscription to a computer bureau in order to share this standby servic[...]
a similar occurrence happened again.

Staff absences

The problem of staff absence is that of prolonged absence of one membe[...]
staff or the absence of a number of staff at one time or absences at crit[...]
periods such as the month end, half year and year end.

The results of the training needs assessment and rescheduling of w[...]
activities should alleviate most of these problems. The staff within [...]
accounting function are now multi-skilled with most tasks able to be d[...]
with by more than one employee. Therefore if for example Mohammed w[...]
on holiday again his sales ledger duties could be covered by Sue and [...]
credit control duties by David without the work of the accounting func[...]
suffering.

The exception to this would be the payroll as there is no member of [...]
accounts clerks staff capable of producing the weekly or monthly pay[...]

owever William Whitelow is capable of running the payroll if this were und to be necessary.

a alternative to covering for staff absences within the accounting function elf is to consider the use of a temporary staff. However a detailed cost-nefit exercise should be carried out before any agreement is entered into.

eview of the accounting system

this section of the report I have considered the current accounting system purchases and supplier payments, sales and customer receipts and payroll d personnel records using a SWOT analysis.

RENGTHS

rchases and supplier payments

all number of suppliers -	personal, partnership type relationship with a limited number of suppliers should ensure better service and quality
ntracts -	contracts are for two/three years resulting in regular review of supplier service
nual price negotiations -	in a climate of low inflation this should prove to be an economical policy
ancial stability checks -	all new suppliers are checked for financial stability by Sue Moran
oice/GRN/order checks -	George Stewart checks all supplier invoices to GRNs, purchase orders and price lists to ensure that what is invoiced is what was ordered and delivered and has been charged at the correct price
ment approval -	Sue Moran identifies suppliers due for monthly payment and these payments are approved by William Whitelow
eque signatories -	all supplier cheques or BACS payments must be signed by William Whitelow and one other director

student notes✍

Sales and customer receipts

Initial cash payment terms -

new customers trade on cash terms for the fi three months

Credit checks -

credit checks on all new customers Mohammed Singh and sales representative

Credit limits -

all new credit limits and changes to credit lim approved by finance director or managi director

Invoicing -

sales invoices sent out daily and compiled fro goods despatched listings

Bankings -

cheque receipts banked daily

Bank reconciliation -

monthly bank reconciliation prepared by Shar Evans and approved by William Whitel (segregation of duties as banking and post carried out by Mohammed Singh)

Aged debtor listing -

produced monthly and reviewed by Willi Whitelow, Elaine Candler and Omar Sangha

Payroll and personnel records

BACS payments -

all monthly pay and 80% of weekly pay p directly into employees' bank accounts by BAC

New system -

integrated payroll and personnel system sho increase efficiency

EAKNESSES

rchases and supplier payments

gotiations - all negotiations and agreements with suppliers are dealt with by George Stewart as are checks on invoices/GRNs/orders - lack of segregation of duties

CS payment - a director's signature is required for BACS payment authority form which is now increasingly used rather than approval of each individual payment

llusion - the whole system is under the control of three employees - George Stewart and William Whitelow who set up the current system and Sue Moran who is George's daughter. The only internal check on the system is the directors' signature on the cheques or BACS form and even this is rarely done by the financial director. Instead it is done by one of the other directors who has little time for or knowledge of independent checks.

es and customer receipts

ne of note

roll and personnel records

ekly payroll - 20% of payments by cash increasing workload, cost and risk of theft

sonnel - Rachel Frey is very new to the company and the system and has only had minimal training on the new system

OPPORTUNITIES

Purchases and supplier payments

New suppliers -   the present policy has been in existence for thr
                               years so the company is now going through t
                               process of renegotiating contracts which m
                               allow new suppliers with better quality/price ir
                               the system and reduce the risk of fraud throu
                               collusion with an existing supplier

Sales and customer receipts

Cash only period -   a review should be carried out as to whether t
                               insistence on the three month cash period
                               initial trading is losing DEL customers

Customer base -   as 16% of customers account for 80% of turnov
                               84% of customers only contribute 20%
                               turnover. Are any of these customers unprofita
                               or is their cost-benefit not worthwhile?

Payroll and personnel records

BACS rather than cash -   some incentive should be given to cash p
                               employees to change to payment through th
                               bank account, and all new employees should
                               paid in this manner

New system -   as both the system and Rachel Frey are new to
                               company the new system may not be being u
                               to its fullest capacity

THREATS

Purchases and supplier payments

Risk of fraud - this is considered in more detail in the next section of this report

Supplier complacency - there is a risk that suppliers on a two/three year contract with DEL may become complacent about price or quality

Sales and customer receipts

None of note

Payroll and personnel records

Risk of theft - there is a risk of theft whilst dealing with cash wages payments

Consideration of potential areas of fraud

After carrying out the SWOT analysis on the accounting system the weakest part of the system is clearly purchases and supplier payments. Following on from this I have carried out a risk assessment exercise using the Ernst and Young matrix model approach.

Details of risk area	Management	Employees	Third parties	Collusion
Contracts		DEL Buyer		Buyer and Supplier
False invoices		DEL Buyer	Supplier	Purchase ledger clerk
Inflated prices		DEL Buyer	Supplier	Purchase ledger clerk
Fictitious supplier		DEL Buyer		Purchase ledger clerk Company Accountant

Risk assessment

Contracts: It is entirely possible that when contracts with suppliers go out for tender specific favoured suppliers could be awarded those contracts despite them not being the best supplier for the company. This could be done by drafting the contract specifications in such a way that they favour one particular supplier or altering the terms of the contract in order to exclude other companies from tendering or to meet the requirements of the favoured supplier. Alternatively once the contracts have been awarded the terms and conditions could be altered suit the favoured supplier.

False invoices: A supplier colludes with the buyer (who checks invoic to GRNs and orders) to produce invoices for goo which were not supplied and DEL then pays for the goods. This would probably require the collusion of t purchase ledger clerk.

Inflated prices: A supplier provides an invoice which is priced too hig in collusion with a buyer who passes the invoice payment. Again this probably requires the collusion the purchase ledger clerk.

Fictitious supplier: The buyer produces false invoices from a fictitio supplier and passes them for payment. This wo probably require the collusion of the purchase led clerk and the company accountant.

Area of risk	Probability	Impact	Controls	Net likely impact	Action
Contracts	High	High	Low	High	Priority
False invoices	Medium	High	Low	Medium	Secon Priority
Inflated prices	Medium	High	Low	Medium	Secon Priority
Fictitious Supplier	Medium	High	Low	Medium	Secon Priorit

The overriding factor here is the low level of internal control throughout purchases and supplier payment system. The only reason that the final th risk areas have a medium priority and therefore medium net likely impa because there would have to be collusion between two or more employees.

A Risk Management Group should be set up in order to review these risk fraud. Once the company's risk appetite has been set then the group r assess the scale of the risk and develop a risk management strategy. composition of this group would most probably be Elaine Candler, fina director as chairman, William Whitelow, as company accountant and m as the accounting systems technician. It would also be a benefit to have other director or manager from outside the accounting function within group in order to bring a different perspective to discussions.

Reporting of issues by colleagues

During a routine meeting to assess the training review and work rescheduling with Mohammed Singh, sales ledger clerk and credit controller, held on 31 March 2003, certain information was brought to my attention. Mohammed mentioned that he had some concerns that there might possibly be an element of fraudulent activity within the purchases and supplier payments system, possibly involving a fictitious or controlled supplier named Raymond Briggs Ltd and three members of DEL's accounting team.

On the basis of the impression that Mohammed gave, rather than any firm evidence, I considered whether I had the authority and expertise to take this matter any further. Given the hospitalisation of yourself and the possible involvement of William Whitelow in the potential fraud, I decided to carry out some preliminary investigations before reporting the matter to you on your return or to the managing director.

Therefore I carried out some preliminary checks of the system in order to determine the full record of DEL's transactions with Raymond Briggs Ltd, details of any credit checks carried out on the company and details of the tendering documentation when Raymond Briggs Ltd tendered for the contract.

Having carried out these limited preliminary checks without alerting any personnel who may be involved with this matter, I will now refer the matter to you and the Board of directors.

Conclusions

Training needs and work rescheduling

In order to reschedule the work activities of the accounting function to ensure more effective use of resources, a variety of training needs have been highlighted. This will help to ensure that the staff in the accounting function are multi-skilled and can therefore carry out more than one function within the system.

Contingency plans

On the basis of recent history, consideration should be given to various contingency plans for either computer failure or staff absences.

Accounting system

The current accounting system has been analysed and it is concluded that there are significant weaknesses and possible areas of fraud within the purchases and supplier payments system. There are also some less serious weaknesses within the payroll and personnel database system but the sales and customer receipts system appears to be sound.

Recommendations

Training and work rescheduling

- significant on the job training should be carried out to ensure that the members of staff in the accounting function can carry out at least one other function other than their main function.

- such training must be followed up by regular scheduling of work so that these new tasks are carried out.

- the tasks of the entire accounting function are to be analysed to determine those which must be carried out at the month and year ends and other tasks and the work of the whole department should be rescheduled on the basis of this timetable.

Contingency plans

- consideration should be given to the setting up of contingency plans for computer failure and problematic staff absences

Purchases and payments system

- segregation of duties within the purchases and payments system should be investigated with division of duties between those receiving goods, maintaining the purchase ledger, authorising the invoices and authorising the payment

- there should be an independent check on the financial stability checks on new suppliers, such as review by the finance director

- all payments, whether by cheque or by BACS should be properly reviewed by the director providing the second signature, or as alternative cheques/BACS forms should be signed by two directors rather than the company accountant and one director

- a purchase ledger control account should be maintained and reconciled to the purchase ledger records by another member of staff such as the Sharon Evans

Payroll system

- incentives should be given to employees currently paid by cash to encourage them to have payment directly into their bank account

- all new employees should automatically be paid by BACS

Potential for fraud

- a risk management group should be set up to review the assessment of the fraud risk within the purchases and supplier payments system and to determine a risk management strategy.

APPENDICES

Appendix 1

Organisation chart and staff competences summary

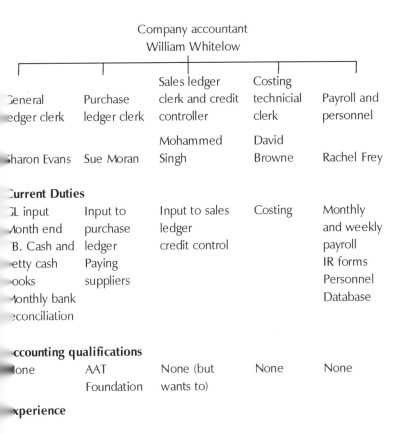

Company accountant
William Whitelow

General ledger clerk	Purchase ledger clerk	Sales ledger clerk and credit controller	Costing technicial clerk	Payroll and personnel
Sharon Evans	Sue Moran	Mohammed Singh	David Browne	Rachel Frey

Current Duties

GL input Month end TB. Cash and petty cash books Monthly bank reconciliation	Input to purchase ledger Paying suppliers	Input to sales ledger credit control	Costing	Monthly and weekly payroll IR forms Personnel Database

Accounting qualifications

None	AAT Foundation	None (but wants to)	None	None

Experience

INDEX

INDEX

ORDER FORM

To: BPP Professional Education, Aldine House, Aldine Place, London, W12 8AW

Mr/Mrs/Ms (name): _____

Daytime delivery address: _____

Postcode: _____   Daytime Tel No: _____

Please send me the following books

	Course Companion	Revision Companion	Combined Companion
Foundation Units 1-4			
Units 1-4	☐ £21.95	☐ £13.95	
Office Skills (Units 21, 22, 23)			☐ £16.95
Intermediate			
Unit 5 Financial Records and Accounts	☐ £14.95	☐ £11.95	
Units 6&7 Cost Information and Reports and Returns	☐ £16.95	☐ £12.95	
Technician			
Units 8&9 Managing Performance and Controlling Resources	☐ £15.95	☐ £12.95	
Unit 10 Managing Accounting Systems and People			☐ £16.95
Unit 11 Drafting Financial Statements	☐ £15.95	☐ £12.95	
Available November 2004			
Unit 15 Cash Management and Control			☐ £16.95
Unit 17 Implementing Auditing Procedures	☐ £15.95	☐ £12.95	
Unit 18 Business Taxation			☐ £16.95
Unit 19 Personal Taxation			☐ £16.95
Postage	☐ £3.00 per book	☐ £3.00 per book	☐ £3.00 per book

(Postage is charged at £3 per book to a maximum of £12)

Total (inc, Postage)   £ _____

I enclose a cheque for _____

or

Please charge my Mastercard / Visa

Card number ☐☐☐☐ ☐☐☐☐ ☐☐☐☐ ☐☐☐☐ ☐☐☐☐

Expiry Date _____   Start Date _____

Issue Number (Switch Only) _____